READY STEADY COOK

fast meals for two

READY STEADY COOK

fast meals for two

BBC

This book is published to accompany the television series
Ready Steady Cook, produced
by Bazal for the BBC.
executive producer: **trevor hyett**
producer: **mary ramsay**
director: **chris fox**

Published by BBC Worldwide Ltd,
Woodlands, 80 Wood Lane, London W12 0TT

First published in 1998

ISBN 0 563 38437 9

commissioning editor: **vivien bowler**
project editor: **rachel brown**
general editor: **orla broderick**
copy editor: **pam mallender**
art director: **ellen wheeler**
design: **balley design associates**
home economist: **sarah ramsbottom**

Set in Gill Sans Light and Bold by Balley Design Associates
Printed in Great Britain by Martins the Printers Limited, Berwick-upon-Tweed
Bound in Great Britain by Hunter & Foulis Limited, Edinburgh
Colour separations by Radstock Reproductions Limted, Midsomer Norton
Cover printed by Belmont Press, Northampton

Recipe illustrated on front cover: *Oriental Beef Salad* (page 71).
Recipes illustrated on back cover (clockwise from top): *Open Mushroom
Lasagne* (page 26), *Potato Cakes with a Niçoise Garnish* (page 30–31)
and *Hot Strawberry and Raspberry Pavlovas* (page 89).

contents

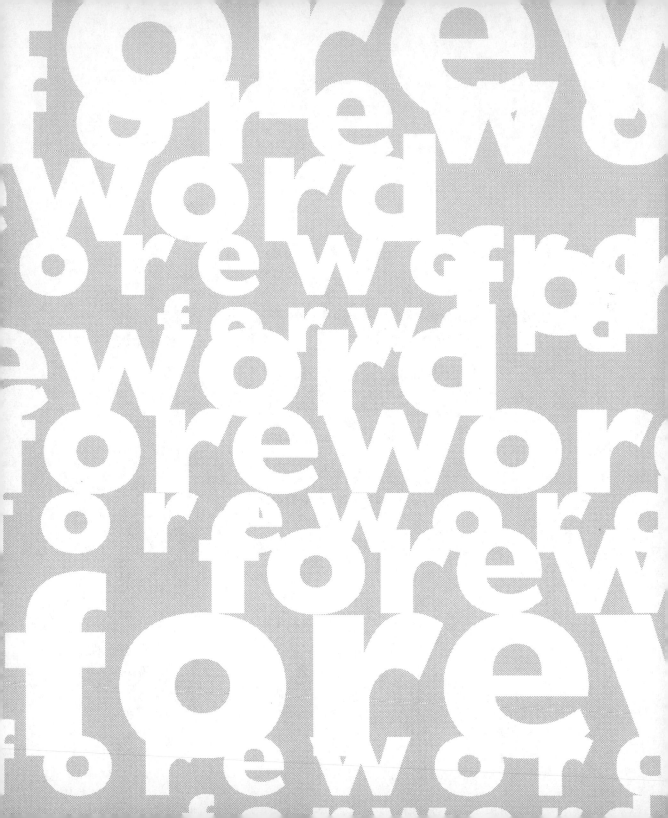

foreword

Welcome to *Ready Steady Cook: Fast Meals for Two*.

If *Ready Steady Cook* the programme has transformed the way you shop, cook and eat, then you're ready for this book!

It's not about special occasion food for several people – it's about giving you the chance to sit down with a loved one or friend and enjoy the pleasure of quick and delicious food *à deux* – for under a fiver! No over-buying and no wasted food at the end.

The most useful thing *Ready Steady Cook* has given me is the ability to shop better. In the olden days (pre *Ready Steady Cook*) I often found that after doing a huge shop, I'd go to the fridge and still find there was nothing to eat! The things I had somehow didn't work together to make a meal – a bit like going to the wardrobe and finding it bulging with clothes, but still having nothing to wear. You get the picture? Now I'm much better at buying a range of ingredients that will work several ways with each other – the food equivalent of a trouser suit, skirt, two blouses and a sarong!

Food is still full of fashion. What was 'in' in the 80s is absolutely 'out' in the 90s. With this book you're ahead of the game – a balance of good traditional tastes with a completely modern approach.

Fresh, exotic and enticing produce from around the world is arriving in our shops in abundance. It is our great fortune that we can experience it. May this book fill you with excitement and inspiration. As Einstein said, 'imagination is more important than knowledge'.

Good luck and love.

x

7

If you're looking for fabulous fast food ideas for two, this *Ready Steady Cook* book is especially for you. And you don't *have* to race round the kitchen to produce the finished dish in 20 minutes; only the chefs on the television programme are put under that pressure! The dishes are, though, deliciously quick to prepare and while a few take slightly longer to cook, the extra wait will be worth it.

Most people at some time will want to cook for just two people. It could be when entertaining a friend or, for many couples, it could be every day. Many cookery books cater for four or even six and it can be confusing and difficult to adjust the recipes.

The exciting new recipes in this book have been designed with this in mind and where they do make more than required, tips are usually given for safe storage or freezing. You can, of course, double or triple the recipes if you are expecting company. But take care, the spices and herbs used

introd

are not automatically increased by two or three times. Add what is specified in the recipe, then taste and gradually add more if needed.

In recent years shopping for smaller quantities has become much easier. Most supermarkets now offer varying sizes of pre-packed meat and fish. Some also have fresh meat and fish counters. In the fresh-produce sections you can choose the size and number of fruit and vegetables that you need and pay for them by weight, so if you plan ahead you can really cut down on waste.

Don't forget, too, your local shops. Butchers and fishmongers will be only too happy to advise on what to buy and don't be worried about asking them to do the jobs they are skilled at, like boning and filleting. It will save you valuable time and if they show you how to do it properly it will come in handy for the next time.

Whether you are looking for a simple supper or lunch, a hearty meal or a candlelit dinner, the *Ready Steady Cook* chefs have come up with a recipe to fit the occasion. Spice up your life with

Richard Cawley's *Tandoori Chicken Skewers with Cucumber Salad* or with a *Thai Green Curry with Prawns and Jasmine Rice* from Patrick Anthony. Take a trip to Hungary with Brian Turner's *Lamb Paprika Goulash* or visit the East with Antony Worrall Thompson and his *Oriental Beef Salad*.

Set fire to the barbecue with *Mackerel Brochettes with Warm Spicy Potato Salad* from Nick Nairn or *Barbecued Lamb with French Bean Salad and Tzatziki* from Ross Burden. There are fishy tales from Paul Rankin with his delicious *Stir-fried Seafood with Chinese Black Beans and Noodles*, and from Nick Nairn with his *Prawn Kedgeree*. Pronto pasta dishes include *Warm Pasta Shells with Chicken, Basil and Pine Nuts* from Phil Vickery who also turns his hand to *Braised Cabbage with Bubbling Goat's Cheese*, just one of many vegetarian dishes.

Making the most of chicken are Kevin Woodford with *Paprika Seared Chicken on a Broccoli Stir-fry*

uction

and Lesley Waters with *Bulgar and Chicken Pilaff with Apricots*.

Whisk up some egg and cheese dishes with Paul Rankin and his *Floating Cheese Soufflés* or try your hand at *Marjoram and Mozzarella Fritters* from Antony Worrall Thompson.

Create a stunning supper with a *Mexican Salsa Pizza* from Lesley Waters or *Lamb Koftas with Baba Ghanoush* from James Martin. And take a walk on the wild side with *Braised Guinea Fowl with Chestnuts* from Richard Cawley or Patrick Anthony's *Rabbit with Apricot and Orange*.

Last, but not least, come mouthwatering desserts made in minutes including an *Apricot Tarte Tatin with Walnut Cream* from James Martin and melting *Hot Strawberry and Raspberry Pavlovas* from Tony Tobin.

Ready Steady Cook is about putting together a delicious dish from whatever ingredients you have to hand. It's also about enjoying yourself in the kitchen. So what are you waiting for? On your marks, get set, go!

a note on ingredients and techniques

You can't make a silk purse out of a sow's ear as the saying goes. And that's equally true when cooking. Quality ingredients make all the difference to the taste of a finished dish.

In an ideal world we would shop daily for fresh produce but in reality this simply is not possible for most of us, so planning ahead is a key ingredient to success. Remember, too, recipes aren't carved in stone; if you find at the last minute you haven't got something, or perhaps you don't even like it, leave it out or substitute a favourite alternative. Don't be afraid to improvise – the *Ready Steady Cook* chefs do it all the time.

Convenience foods play an important part in the majority of these recipes, providing valuable short-cuts which save you time and effort with no loss of flavour. It's a good idea to keep some on stand-by in your store-cupboard, fridge or freezer. Shortcrust and puff pastry now come fresh and frozen in ready-rolled sheets, frozen vegetables offer as much food value as fresh, and canned pulses and beans mean no more overnight soaking. Fresh and dried pasta in its many forms also provides a good starting point for a tasty supper.

Canned chopped tomatoes are a real boon in the winter months when expensive imported fresh tomatoes can turn out to be both colourless and flavourless. Substitute for fresh in cooked dishes (one heaped tablespoon of chopped is the equivalent of a medium-sized fresh tomato).

On the subject of cans and packets, manufacturers do not always work to the same metric weights. Simply find the closest one to the recipe you are following. For example, there is a negligible difference between a 397 g and 400 g can and the dish will not be spoiled by using either one.

Fresh herbs are by far the best for flavour but frozen make an excellent alternative. Buy pots of fresh herbs, then freeze those not used or invest in tubs of quick-frozen herbs which can be used straight from the freezer. If you do opt for dried, or the recipe specifies them, freeze-dried herbs tend to come out on top in the taste test. Remember if you are substituting dried herbs for fresh, use only half the quantity – they are much more concentrated.

Ready-ground spices have such a short shelf-life it's a good idea to buy whole spices and grind as needed, using a pestle and mortar. If you don't have a pestle and mortar, place them in a bowl and use the end of a rolling pin.

Grated hard cheeses, such as Cheddar or Parmesan, freeze well and may be used from frozen in sauces and hot dishes. Remember, too, that you can freeze individual portions of food if you have some over, or want to plan ahead.

Chocolate quality varies considerably and the

finest always contains a high proportion of cocoa butter. Look for bars containing at least 50 per cent cocoa solids when you are planning to make one of those desserts to die for.

If you've gone teetotal or don't like alcohol, you can always substitute stock in savoury recipes and fresh fruit juice in sweet dishes. But if you *are* using wine, use one you would enjoy drinking, rather than a cheap 'cooking' wine which will undoubtedly spoil all your hard work. If it's not worth drinking, it's not worth cooking with. And if you're not planning to drink the remainder you can always buy small ring-pull cans.

Some of the recipes contain lightly cooked eggs. Because of the slight risk of salmonella poisoning, these should be avoided by pregnant women and the sick, elderly, and very young. These dishes should only be made from absolutely fresh eggs from a reliable source.

If you are trying to cut calories or reduce the fat in your diet it doesn't mean you have to miss out. Check out some healthy alternatives. Buy trimmed or extra-lean meat and bacon and remove the skin from chicken pieces. Use half-fat hard cheeses and semi-skimmed milk. For everyday, try low-fat fromage frais and low-fat natural yoghurt as substitutes for cream and crème fraîche. Opt for low-fat soft cheese instead of cream cheese. Cook with sunflower, vegetable or olive oil in place of butter where possible.

- **When cooking any of the recipes, stick to one set of measurements – metric or imperial. They are not interchangeable.**
- **Eggs are medium. If your kitchen is warm, keep the eggs in the fridge, but allow them to come to room temperature before using them.**
- **Wash all fresh produce before preparation and peel as necessary.**
- **Spoon measurements are level. Always use proper measuring spoons: 1 teaspoon = 5 ml; 1 dessertspoon = 10 ml; 1 tablespoon = 15 ml.**

The chefs on *Ready Steady Cook* often cook on a ridged cast-iron griddle pan with a spout for pouring off the cooking juices. Not only is it more healthy to cook this way as little or no fat is used, but it also gives a professional criss-cross charred look to food. Heat until very hot before adding steaks, chops, fish or chunky slices of vegetables. To achieve the attractive grill-marks, give the food a half-turn half-way through cooking each side. An ovenproof frying pan is also a good investment as it can be transferred from the hob straight into the oven or under the grill to finish off a dish.

A good chopping board will certainly save your work surfaces and if you have two boards all the better. If you do not have two, remember never to prepare raw fish, poultry or meat on a board, then use the same side or utensils for cutting cooked food or food that is being eaten raw. Scrub the board between uses, or do as the chefs do and turn it over.

who's who in *ready steady cook*

Patrick Anthony

Food writer and broadcaster Patrick has now earned himself a loyal following among the *Ready Steady Cook* viewers eager to learn about his latest gadgetry discovery. He is also a regular contributor to BBC's *Food and Drink* programme where he is affectionately known as Captain Gadget.

Ross Burden

New Zealand-born Ross has many accolades to his name, including being credited by *Company Magazine* as one of London's most eligible bachelors! Ross is self-taught and first began his television career when he reached the final of BBC's *Masterchef* programme. He is currently working on his first book.

Richard Cawley

Richard's artistic temperament is evident in both his cookery and his flamboyant dress. He trained at art school and was happy to turn his creativity to food. Richard thoroughly enjoys *Ready Steady Cook* and is usually found competing alongside his regular opponent Patrick Anthony. He has recently fulfilled a lifelong ambition, appearing as the dame in his first pantomime.

James Martin

Ready Steady Cook's newest and youngest recruit, James is a big hit with the programme's student viewers. Although aged just 24, James has already appeared on *Food and Drink* and many other television programmes. He is currently working on his first book and plans to open his own bistro and bakery very soon.

Nick Nairn

Scotland's youngest Michelin-starred chef, Nick Nairn has a fast and furious pace that keeps the *Ready Steady Cook* contestants on their toes. Nick has recently opened a new restaurant in Glasgow, Nairns, and has also released a new television series, *Island Harvest*, which has an accompanying BBC book.

Paul Rankin

Along with his wife Jeanne, chef Paul Rankin has been awarded Northern Ireland's first ever Michelin Star. Their restaurant, Roscoff, was also named Restaurant of the Year at the BBC *Good Food* Awards. He has travelled across the globe gaining insights into Japanese and Asian food that are evident in his *Ready Steady Cook* recipes.

Tony Tobin

Training under Nico Ladenis for several years, Tony Tobin has learned to cook classical French food under one of the world's most famous classical French chefs. Currently appearing on *Ready Steady Cook*, Tony is the Head Chef at the Dining Room in Reigate, Surrey and is working on his first book. He also owns a restaurant chain, Tortellini, which has branches throughout Surrey and Sussex.

Brian Turner

One of *Ready Steady Cook*'s original team, Brian is still very much a 'hands-on' chef at his own restaurant, Turner's, in London's Chelsea. He developed his classical style of cookery in many top-ranking kitchens including Simpsons in the Strand and the Beau Rivage Palace in Switzerland. Brian is now a regular on ITV's *This Morning* and is also involved in a new chain of high street restaurants called Orange Balloon.

Phil Vickery

Head chef and Director of the acclaimed Castle Hotel, Phil Vickery is carving out a name for himself as one of Britain's most talented chefs and television personalities. He has just won the Egon Ronay Chef of the Year Award 1998 and has recently opened a new brasserie and bar called Brazz.

Lesley Waters

Her lively personality makes Lesley Waters one of television's most popular female chefs. Her varied career includes working as head teacher at Leith's School of Food and Wine in London, writing several books and working part-time as an aerobics teacher. Leslie now appears regularly on BBC's *Food and Drink* programme and co-presents ITV's *Surprise Chefs*. She has just published a new book, *Broader than Beans* (Headline).

Kevin Woodford

A member of the original *Ready Steady Cook* team and a regular face on television, Kevin is the star of several programmes including BBC's *Can't Cook Won't Cook* and *The Holiday Programme*. Kevin is also co-owner of the prestigious Waterfront Restaurant, which overlooks Douglas Bay on the Isle of Man.

Antony Worrall Thompson

Antony's colourful career as cookery expert not only embraces his television work, but has also incorporated being head chef and proprietor of many award-winning restaurants. He and his wife have now opened their own restaurant, Woz, in west London where he is frequently found behind the stoves. Antony has recently become the new resident chef on BBC's popular *Food and Drink* programme.

sweetcorn and sweet potato chowder by phil vickery

4 tablespoons of olive oil

2 red onions, finely chopped

1 sweet potato, diced

2 celery sticks, thinly sliced (reserve leaves for garnish)

1 small or ½ a large corn on the cob, kernels removed

½ teaspoon chopped fresh rosemary

½ vegetable stock cube

120 ml (4 fl oz) milk

1–2 tablespoons olive oil, for brushing

½ French stick, cut into four slices

1 garlic clove, halved

Salt and freshly ground black pepper

hot tips

● If you can't get sweet potatoes, use an ordinary potato. You can also use frozen or drained, canned sweetcorn if fresh corn on the cob is out of season.

● Vegetable stock can be very time-consuming to make. If you are using stock cubes read the packet and check that they do not contain flavour, preservatives or enhancers. Your chowder will taste all the better for not containing them.

You could also try serving this soup with garlic croutons. Simply toss together cubes of country-style bread with crushed garlic, seasoning and a little olive oil. Spread out on a baking sheet and bake in an oven pre-heated to gas mark 7, 220°C (425°F) for 5–10 minutes or until golden brown and crispy.

❶ Pre-heat the oven to gas mark 7, 220°C (425°F). Heat 2 tablespoons of the oil in a large pan, add the onions and gently fry for a few minutes until softened. Add the sweet potato, celery, corn kernels and rosemary, stirring to coat. Sweat for 5 minutes.

❷ Add 500 ml (18 fl oz) of water to the pan and crumble in the stock cube. Bring to a gentle simmer and cook until all the vegetables are tender. Hand-blend leaving the mixture chunky. Add the milk and reheat gently. Season to taste.

❸ Brush an ovenproof griddle pan with some of the olive oil and heat until smoking hot. Rub the bread slices with the garlic halves and drizzle the remaining olive oil over them. Bake for 5–6 minutes.

❹ Meanwhile, deep-fry the celery leaves until crisp and golden. Ladle the soup into bowls, garnish with the deep-fried celery leaves and serve hot with the warm bruschetta.

floating cheese soufflés

by paul rankin

15 g (½ oz) unsalted butter, plus extra for
greasing
1 tablespoon plain flour
50 ml (2 fl oz) milk
Pinch of freshly grated nutmeg
3 eggs
300 ml (10 fl oz) double cream
50 g (2 oz) Gruyère cheese, finely grated
50 g (2 oz) Cheddar, grated
Salt and freshly ground black pepper
Chopped fresh chives, to garnish

hot tip

● Use a mature Cheddar when making
these special soufflés. Made from
pasteurized cows' milk, Cheddar has a
hard, sometimes crumbly texture and its
colour deepens with age. Its taste ranges
from sweet and fresh in young cheese to
rich and nutty the longer it matures. It has
particularly good melting qualities.

**I had to make hundreds of these soufflés during
my days at a well-known London restaurant, Le
Gavroche. They were, and still are, among its
most popular dishes.**

❶ Pre-heat the oven to gas mark 6, 200°C (400°F). Butter two
12 cm (5 in) squares of greaseproof paper and place on a
buttered baking sheet.

❷ Place the butter, flour and milk in a small pan and bring to the
boil, whisking continuously. Reduce the heat, add the nutmeg and
season to taste. Simmer for another 2–3 minutes until you have
a smooth thick sauce. Remove from the heat.

❸ Separate the eggs. Place the whites in a large bowl and whisk
until stiff peaks form. Stir two of the yolks into the sauce. Remove
1 tablespoon of the sauce, cover and set aside.

❹ Transfer the remaining sauce to a large bowl and using a large
whisk or metal spoon, fold in a third of the egg whites to loosen
the mixture, then carefully fold in the remainder. Divide the
mixture between the buttered squares and bake for 5–6 minutes
until well risen and firm to the touch.

❺ Meanwhile, heat the cream in an ovenproof frying pan and
season generously. Whisk in the reserved sauce and bring to a
gentle simmer. Remove the soufflés from the oven and carefully tip
them into the cream. Spoon some of the cream on top of each
one, then sprinkle with the Gruyère and Cheddar. Return the frying
pan to the oven and bake for 5 minutes or until the soufflés are
puffed up and lightly golden. Transfer into serving bowls and spoon
around the sauce. Garnish with chopped chives and serve at once.

asparagus custards

by antony worrall thompson

Knob of unsalted butter, for greasing
100 g (4 oz) asparagus spears
200 ml (7 fl oz) double cream
1 small garlic clove, crushed
½ teaspoon snipped fresh chives
½ teaspoon chopped fresh chervil
1 teaspoon chopped fresh flatleaf parsley
2 eggs
Salt and freshly ground white pepper

These are basically savoury crème caramels with a delicate and fresh summer flavour. Serve as a starter or as a light supper with a crisp green salad and crusty French bread.

❶ Pre-heat the oven to gas mark 2, 150°C (300°F). Butter two 150 ml (5 fl oz) ramekins. Cut the asparagus leaving a 4 cm (1½ in) tip, then cut each tip into four lengthways and set them aside. Slice the remaining asparagus and plunge into a pan of boiling water for 2 minutes, then drain and refresh under cold running water.

❷ Place the cream in a pan with the garlic and boil to reduce to 150 ml (5 fl oz). Pour into a food processor and add the blanched asparagus and all the herbs. Whizz until smooth. Break the eggs into a bowl and lightly whisk, then add the cream mixture and stir until well combined. Season to taste and strain through a sieve into a jug.

❸ Divide the reserved asparagus tips between the ramekins. Pour over the egg and cream mixture and place the ramekins in a small roasting tin. Pour enough boiling water into the tin to come half-way up the sides of the ramekins. Bake for 25–30 minutes until the custards are just set. Remove from the oven, leave to stand for 5 minutes, then unmould to serve.

hot tip

● The correct term for cooking food indirectly over water is a *bain marie*. The term *bain marie* is often thought to refer to the Virgin Mary, the symbol of gentleness, suggesting the gentleness of this method of cooking. A *bain marie* is used for keeping sauces or soups warm, for melting ingredients without burning them and for cooking dishes very slowly.

marjoram and mozzarella fritters

by antony worrall thompson

2 x 150 g (5 oz) balls mozzarella
(buffalo, if possible), drained and grated
200 g (7 oz) Parmesan, freshly grated
1 egg
2 tablespoons plain flour
1 tablespoon chopped fresh marjoram
1 garlic clove, finely chopped
½ red chilli, seeded and finely chopped
Olive oil, for frying
Salt and freshly ground black pepper
Fresh herb sprigs, to garnish

These are extremely moreish and you'll find that they disappear in minutes. Try to buy good quality mozzarella as it makes all the difference, and cook the fritters straight from the fridge for best results.

❶ Place the mozzarella in a bowl with the Parmesan, egg, flour, marjoram, garlic and chilli. Season to taste and gently fold the ingredients together. Shape the mixture into about fourteen 2.5 cm (1 in) balls and arrange on a plate. Chill for at least 10 minutes or up to 24 hours covered in the fridge.
❷ Make the spicy tomato sauce.
❸ Heat at least 5 cm (2 in) of oil in a large pan or deep-fat fryer to 190°C (375°F). Add a few of the mozzarella balls and deep-fry in batches for 2–3 minutes or until golden. Drain on kitchen paper. Garnish a serving plate with herb sprigs, add the mozzarella fritters and serve with the sauce.

...with spicy tomato sauce

2 tablespoons olive oil

1 red onion, finely chopped

1 large garlic clove, crushed

400 g (14 oz) can chopped tomatoes in rich tomato juice

1 tablespoon tomato purée

1 tablespoon chopped mixed fresh herbs, such as flatleaf parsley, basil and thyme

½ red chilli, seeded and finely chopped

Salt and freshly ground black pepper

❶ Heat a small pan and add the oil. Add the onion and garlic and cook for a few minutes until softened but not coloured. Add the tomatoes, tomato purée, herbs, chilli and seasoning and simmer gently for 10–15 minutes until the sauce is reduced and thickened. Transfer to a serving dish.

hot tip

● Mozzarella is an Italian curd cheese, white, spongy and egg-shaped, and is usually found packed in brine. It has a mild, creamy-sour flavour. The best is traditionally made from water buffaloes' milk and is worth searching out. It has a lovely texture and taste. Nowadays, though, mozzarella is more commonly made from cows' milk.

fried halloumi cheese with greek salad and vinaigrette by tony tobin

1 red onion, thinly sliced

1 tablespoon white-wine vinegar

1 dessertspoon each of chopped fresh basil,

chervil, coriander and snipped chives

5 tablespoons olive oil

4 ripe plum tomatoes, cut into large dice

1 cucumber, peeled and cut into large dice

20 pitted black olives

1 tablespoon chopped fresh

flatleaf parsley

150 g (5 oz) halloumi cheese, thinly sliced

2 tablespoons fresh lemon juice

Salt and freshly ground black pepper

Halloumi is a Greek semi-hard cheese with a creamy, slightly salty taste. It can be found in the chill cabinets of large supermarkets and needs to be eaten hot as, once it cools, it's a bit like chewing rubber!

❶ Place the onion in a non-metallic bowl with the vinegar and marinate for 5 minutes. In another bowl, mix together the basil, chervil, coriander and chives with 3 tablespoons of olive oil to make a vinaigrette.

❷ Make the salad: place the tomatoes, cucumber, olives, and the onion and vinegar mixture in a bowl. Add the remaining oil and the parsley, season generously and mix well.

❸ Heat a non-stick pan until very hot. Fry the halloumi cheese until brown on both sides (this will take about 30 seconds each side). Remove from the pan, season with pepper, then sprinkle with 1 dessertspoon of the lemon juice.

❹ Add the remaining lemon juice to the herb and oil mixture to finish the vinaigrette.

❺ Place a spoonful of salad into the centre of each plate, top with a few slices of the halloumi, then drizzle round the vinaigrette to serve.

hot tip

● To accompany the halloumi, why not try making some garlic pitta fingers? Simply grill a pitta bread on one side, turn it over and brush with a little melted butter. Sprinkle over some chopped herbs and garlic and grill until the topping is bubbling. Cut into fingers and serve.

garlic mushroom parcels

by tony tobin

1 x 375 g (13 oz) packet ready-rolled puff
pastry, thawed if frozen

2–3 tablespoons mild wholegrain mustard

1 tablespoon olive oil and knob of
unsalted butter, for frying

1 small onion, finely chopped

2 garlic cloves, crushed

225 g (8 oz) chestnut mushrooms, sliced

Small bunch of fresh flatleaf parsley,
roughly chopped

Fresh lemon juice

1 egg, beaten

150 ml (5 fl oz) double cream

Sea salt and freshly ground black pepper

Fresh flatleaf parsley sprigs, to garnish

hot tips

● If you are not a fan of mustard, sprinkle
finely chopped fresh mixed herbs or
freshly grated Parmesan on the pastry.

● Fresh flatleaf parsley is more pungent
than the curly variety and brings out the
true flavour of the mushrooms.

You could use a selection of mushrooms for this recipe. There is no need to wash commercially produced ones as they are grown on sterile material. Just a quick wipe with a damp cloth will do if needed.

❶ Pre-heat the oven to gas mark 7, 220°C (425°F). Unroll the pastry on to a lightly floured surface and brush over 1 heaped tablespoon of mustard. Fold the pastry in half to enclose the mustard and roll out again as thinly as possible. Cut out two 25 cm (10 in) squares and leave to rest.

❷ Heat the olive oil and butter in a frying pan. Add the onion, garlic and mushrooms to the pan and fry until softened. Stir in the parsley, season and add a squeeze of lemon juice. Remove from the heat and cool slightly.

❸ Pile the garlic mushrooms into the middle of the pastry squares. Draw up the edges of each square and squeeze them together to seal. Trim the tops flat. Turn the parcels over and gently press into lightly oiled 10 cm (4 in) fluted tartlet tins (you can also use Yorkshire pudding tins). Brush with beaten egg, sprinkle with a little salt and place on a baking sheet. Bake for 8–10 minutes or until puffed up and golden brown.

❹ Place the cream in a small pan with 2 teaspoons of mustard. Season and heat gently to thicken. Remove the tartlet tins from the oven and carefully turn out the parcels. Arrange them on serving plates, drizzle round the sauce and garnish with parsley sprigs to serve.

21

marinated vegetables with roasted pepper oil by phil vickery

1 small red and 1 small yellow pepper, seeded and roughly chopped
2 garlic cloves, peeled
150 ml (5 fl oz) olive oil, plus 2 tablespoons
1 courgette, cut into 2 cm (¾ in) slices
1 small fennel bulb, trimmed and cut into 4 pieces lengthways
2 small carrots, cut into 2 cm (¾ in) thick slices
1 small aubergine, cut into 2 cm (¾ in) pieces
3 tablespoons fresh lemon juice
1 dessertspoon each of chopped fresh basil, tarragon, thyme and rosemary
Knob of unsalted butter
2 flat mushrooms, sliced
1 small cooked beetroot (not in vinegar), cut into 2 cm (¾ in) cubes
Salt and freshly ground black pepper
1 tablespoon chopped fresh flatleaf parsley, to garnish
Crusty bread, to serve (optional)

The roasted pepper oil will keep in the fridge in a screw-topped jar or bottle for up to a week. Just allow it to come back to room temperature and shake well before using.

❶ Pre-heat the oven to gas mark 5, 190°C (375°F). Place the peppers and the garlic in an ovenproof dish, cover with 150 ml (5 fl oz) of olive oil and bake for about 40 minutes or until the peppers have coloured slightly and are tender when pierced with the point of a sharp knife.

❷ Place the courgette, fennel, carrots and aubergine in an ovenproof dish with 1 tablespoon of lemon juice and 2 tablespoons of olive oil. Season generously and mix well. Bake for 30 minutes or until the vegetables are just tender, then remove from the heat and leave to cool.

❸ Stir the basil, tarragon, thyme and rosemary and remaining lemon juice into the pepper mixture. Season generously and marinate for at least 5 minutes or up to 2 hours. When the oil has cooled, pass through a sieve, discard the peppers and reserve the oil. Season to taste.

❹ Melt the butter in a frying pan and cook the mushrooms over a high heat for 2–3 minutes. Divide the beetroot and mushrooms between two serving plates and pile the roasted vegetables on top, drizzle with the pepper oil and sprinkle with the parsley. Serve at room temperature with some crusty bread, if liked.

caramelized onion and goat's cheese frittata by antony worrall thompson

3 tablespoons olive oil

40 g (1½ oz) unsalted butter

2 large sweet onions, sliced

Pinch of sugar

½ teaspoon fresh thyme leaves

2 garlic cloves, crushed

6 eggs

25 g (1 oz) Parmesan, freshly grated

½ teaspoon chopped fresh sage

100 g (4 oz) mild, creamy goat's cheese, crumbled

Salt and freshly ground black pepper

Fresh herb sprigs, to garnish

hot tip

● If you don't like goat's cheese, use a cheese that melts well such as Cheddar, Gruyère or Emmental to top the frittata.

A frittata is thicker and more substantial than an omelette. To make a really good frittata, the secret is to cook it over a constant low heat in a heavy-based frying pan.

❶ Heat a heavy-based pan and add 2 tablespoons of oil and 25 g (1 oz) of butter. Add the onions and sprinkle with the sugar. Cook, stirring occasionally, for at least 10 minutes and up to 30 minutes until the onions are caramelized. Season and add the thyme and garlic 5 minutes before the end of cooking time. Stir to combine. Tip into a bowl and leave to cool.

❷ Place the eggs in a large bowl with the Parmesan and sage. Tip in the cooled onions, season generously and beat lightly together. Heat a non-stick, heavy-based frying pan, then add the remaining oil and butter and swirl to coat.

❸ Pre-heat the grill. Pour the egg mixture into the frying pan and cook for 2 minutes over a low heat to set the bottom and sides. Scatter over the goat's cheese and cook for 5–10 minutes or until just set.

❹ Flash the frittata under the grill until the cheese is bubbling and lightly golden. Slip it out on to a serving plate and cut into wedges. Garnish with herb sprigs and serve warm or cold.

veggie mushroom burgers

by ross burden

8 x 10 cm (4 in) wide flat mushrooms,
stems removed
2 tablespoons olive oil
225 g (8 oz) soft goat's cheese
1 teaspoon chopped fresh thyme
2 garlic cloves, crushed
Salt and freshly ground black pepper
Fresh flatleaf parsley sprigs, to garnish

A delicious combination of mushrooms stuffed with creamy goat's cheese, this makes a meat-free meal full of interesting flavours and textures. It's a perfect dish for the barbecue.

❶ Heat a griddle pan until smoking hot. Trim the mushrooms to uniform shapes. Brush with some of the olive oil and place, gill-side down, in the pan. Cook the mushrooms for 5 minutes or until the gills are just tender, but do not turn them.

❷ In a bowl, mash together the goat's cheese, thyme and garlic and season generously.

❸ Remove the mushrooms from the heat and brush all over with the remaining oil. Fill four of them with the goat's cheese mixture, then place the remaining mushrooms on top to form sandwiches. Place the 'burgers' back in the pan. Cook, turning occasionally, for 3–4 minutes, or until the cheese starts to melt. Garnish with parsley sprigs to serve.

hot tips

● These burgers can be made in advance, up to the sandwich stage. To finish them off, pop them in a griddle pan or on the side of the barbecue.

● You can substitute any soft cream cheese for the goat's cheese if you prefer.

baked four-cheese pasta

by paul rankin

225 g (8 oz) dried macaroni or penne

50 g (2 oz) unsalted butter,
plus extra for greasing

2 tablespoons light olive oil

100 g (4 oz) tender young spinach leaves

175 g (6 oz) button mushrooms,
quartered

1 tablespoon plain flour

250 ml (8 fl oz) milk

150 ml (5 fl oz) double cream

50 g (2 oz) Stilton, Roquefort
or Gorgonzola, crumbled

50 g (2 oz) Gruyère, Emmental
or Cheddar, grated

50 g (2 oz) mozzarella or Brie, thinly sliced

50 g (2 oz) Parmesan, grana or
pecorino, grated

Salt and freshly ground black pepper

This dish is great for using the left-overs from a cheeseboard as you only really need a small amount of each cheese. You can flash the dish under the grill, if you are short of time, instead of baking it in the oven.

❶ Pre-heat the oven to gas mark 5, 190°C (375°F). Place the pasta in a pan of boiling salted water, stir once and cook for 8–10 minutes, or according to packet instructions, until *al dente*.

❷ Heat 15 g (½ oz) of butter and half the oil in a frying pan. Add the spinach, season generously and cook for a few minutes, tossing occasionally, until wilted. Tip into a sieve set over a bowl. When the spinach has cooled a little, squeeze out any excess water, using your hands.

❸ Add 15 g (½ oz) of butter and the remaining oil to the pan and cook the mushrooms over a high heat for 2–3 minutes. Season generously.

❹ Place the remaining butter in a pan with the flour and milk and bring to the boil, whisking constantly. Reduce the heat and cook, stirring occasionally, for 2–3 minutes until the sauce is smooth and thickened. Season to taste and stir in the cream.

❺ Drain the pasta and refresh under cold running water. Return to the pan and add the spinach, mushrooms, white sauce and two-thirds of the cheeses. Toss until well combined, then tip into a lightly buttered baking dish. Scatter over the remaining cheeses and bake for 15–20 minutes until bubbling and lightly golden.

open mushroom lasagne

by phil vickery

150 ml (5 fl oz) white wine

1 dessertspoon white-wine vinegar

Pinch of sugar

1 onion, chopped

1 tablespoon double cream

75 g (3 oz) unsalted butter, diced and chilled

3 tablespoons olive oil

1 garlic clove, crushed

1 long red chilli, seeded and finely chopped

1 tablespoon chopped fresh coriander

200 g (7 oz) packet mixed fresh wild mushrooms, roughly chopped

6 fresh lasagne sheets

200 g (7 oz) curly kale or Savoy cabbage, stalks removed and roughly chopped

Salt and freshly ground black pepper

Fresh parsley sprigs, to garnish

If you have dried lasagne to hand, cook according to the packet instructions, or until *al dente*, then cool under cold running water. When you are ready to assemble the dish, simply rinse the pasta in hot water before using.

❶ Heat the white wine, white-wine vinegar, sugar and half the onion in a small pan and reduce the liquid by two-thirds. Add the cream, then whisk in 50 g (2 oz) of butter, season and simmer gently until just combined.

❷ Place 1 tablespoon of oil in a large frying pan or wok. Fry the remaining onion for a few minutes until softened. Add the garlic, chilli and coriander and cook for 2 minutes. Add the remaining oil to the frying pan, then add the mushrooms and sauté over a high heat for 2–3 minutes or until the mushrooms are tender.

❸ Meanwhile, bring two large pans of salted water to the boil. Place the lasagne sheets in one pan and simmer for about 2 minutes, or until *al dente*, then drain. Place the kale or Savoy cabbage in the other pan and cook for 2 minutes, then drain well. Transfer the kale or cabbage to a frying pan, add the remaining butter, season with salt and warm through until the butter melts.

❹ Divide the kale or cabbage between two warmed wide-rimmed serving bowls, top with a lasagne sheet, then add a spoonful of the mushroom mixture. Continue layering until all the ingredients are used up, then spoon over the sauce and garnish with parsley sprigs to serve.

hot tip

● Kale, a member of the cabbage family, is a leafy winter vegetable that does not form a heart. Curly kale is the most widely available and has quite a pronounced flavour.

chilli noodles with wilted greens

by lesley waters

1 tablespoon sunflower oil, plus
1 teaspoon
100 g (4 oz) packet carrot batons, or
2 large carrots, cut into batons
100 g (4 oz) packet small cauliflower florets
100 g (4 oz) medium egg noodles
2 teaspoons medium curry powder
3 tablespoons crunchy peanut butter
1 tablespoon tomato purée
1 tablespoon dark soy sauce
100 g (4 oz) spring greens,
roughly chopped
1 teaspoon sesame oil

Peanut butter is always to be found in my store-cupboard and makes an excellent base for a hot, nutty sauce. Here it is tossed with vegetables and sizzling noodles to make a speedy, spicy supper.

❶ Heat a large wok. Add 1 tablespoon of oil, then tip in the carrots and cauliflower florets. Stir-fry for 1 minute, reduce the heat slightly, cover and cook for 3–4 minutes until the vegetables are just tender.

❷ Meanwhile, cook the noodles according to packet instructions. Place the remaining teaspoon of oil and the curry powder in a microwave proof bowl and cook in the microwave on high for 1 minute. Stir in the peanut butter, tomato purée, soy sauce and 150 ml (5 fl oz) of water. Cook on high for 2–3 minutes, stirring once half-way through cooking, until thickened and bubbling (you could cook the sauce in a small pan over a gentle heat, stirring occasionally, for about 5 minutes).

❸ Add the spring greens to the wok and stir-fry for 1 minute until they are well mixed with the other vegetables. Drain the noodles and toss with the sesame oil. Divide the noodles between two shallow bowls and spoon over the stir-fried vegetables. Top with a large spoonful of the hot sauce and toss together. Serve any remaining sauce separately.

spinach and ricotta mezzaluna with sage butter by ross burden

FOR THE PASTA

150 g (5 oz) plain flour

4 egg yolks

1 teaspoon milk

FOR THE FILLING

100 g (4 oz) frozen spinach, thawed, squeezed dry and finely chopped

100 g (4 oz) ricotta

2 tablespoons freshly grated Parmesan, plus shavings to garnish

Pinch of freshly grated nutmeg

FOR THE SAGE BUTTER

40 g (1½ oz) unsalted butter

1 tablespoon chopped fresh sage

Salt and freshly ground black pepper

The mezzaluna can be blanched in boiling water for 1 minute, dunked into cold water, drained and oiled, then kept in the fridge for a couple of hours – not more or they will go slimy. Dunk again in boiling water to reheat.

❶ Place the flour, egg yolks and milk in a food processor and process for 1 minute until the mixture resembles fine breadcrumbs. Transfer on to a work surface and work the mixture together, then knead briefly to form a smooth dough. Wrap in plastic film and leave to rest for up to 1 hour in the fridge.

❷ Make the filling: combine the spinach, ricotta and Parmesan, then season with the nutmeg and salt and pepper.

❸ Cut the dough in half and flour well. Feed through the largest setting of a pasta machine. Fold in half and pass through again, sprinkling with more flour if sticky. Set the rollers one setting thinner and pass the dough through. Fold in half and pass through again. Repeat for the next setting.

❹ Using a 6 cm (2½ in) pastry cutter, stamp out 18–20 pasta circles. Spoon a small heap of the spinach stuffing on to each circle. Moisten the edges with a little water and fold each pasta circle in half, pressing the edges to seal.

❺ Make the sage butter: gently heat the butter and sage in a pan until the sage begins to crisp slightly.

❻ Bring a large pan of salted water to the boil. Plunge the mezzaluna into the water and cook for 1½–2 minutes or until they rise to the surface. Remove with a slotted spoon and drain well. Divide between two warmed wide-rimmed serving bowls and pour over the sage butter. Grind over black pepper and garnish with Parmesan shavings.

hot tip

● Fresh home-made pasta is a special treat and not hard to make. For an authentic pasta, you can use double zero flour, otherwise known as farino 00, which is made from specially refined durum wheat. It produces a good stiff pasta. Plain flour tends to produce a softer texture.

braised cabbage with bubbling goat's cheese by phil vickery

175 g (6 oz) dried tagliatelle
50g (2 oz) walnut pieces
50 g (2 oz) unsalted butter
3–4 tablespoons extra virgin olive oil
1 red onion, cut into thin slivers
½ Savoy cabbage, shredded
1 large garlic clove
120 g (4½ oz) packet goat's cheese,
halved horizontally
Sea salt and freshly ground black pepper

hot tip

● If the thought of cabbage fills you with awful memories of schooldays past, substitute Swiss chard, which is related to the spinach family. Choose fresh looking bulbs with unblemished ribs and crisp leaves and wash well in several changes of water before using. You could also use ordinary spinach.

If you don't want to switch on the oven especially to toast the walnuts, they can be successfully roasted under a hot grill. Place in a hot, dry, non-stick frying pan and keep an eye on them.

❶ Pre-heat the oven to gas mark 7, 220°C (425°F). Plunge the pasta into a large pan of boiling salted water and cook for 8–10 minutes, or until *al dente*, then drain and refresh under cold running water.

❷ Toast the walnuts in the oven for 2–3 minutes on a baking tray.

❸ Heat the butter and a little olive oil in a sauté pan, then add half the onion slivers. Cook for a few minutes until softened. Add the cabbage to the pan and braise for a few minutes. Spoon out a little of the butter and place in a blender with the walnuts, garlic, 1 tablespoon of olive oil and plenty of sea salt. Whizz until just combined to make a pesto.

❹ Pre-heat the grill to hot. Brush a griddle pan with a little oil and char-grill the remaining onion slivers for 1–2 minutes on each side. Drizzle the goat's cheese with olive oil and season, then place on a baking sheet and grill for 1 minute or until just bubbling.

❺ Divide the cabbage between two serving bowls and stir in a couple of tablespoons of the walnut pesto. Top with the pasta drizzled with the remaining pesto. Sit the goat's cheese on top, then garnish with the char-grilled onion slivers to serve.

potato cakes with a niçoise
garnish by tony tobin

2 potatoes, well scrubbed and diced

1 small onion, finely chopped

Olive oil, for frying

1 small red chilli, finely chopped

1 teaspoon mixed dried herbs

100 g (4 oz) can pitted olives, drained and chopped

6 basil leaves, torn

4 small vine-ripened tomatoes, seeded and chopped

1 egg yolk

Plain flour, seasoned with salt and pepper

Salt and freshly ground black pepper

This Mediterranean-inspired dish offers a huge range of flavours and textures. It can be simplified by omitting the Niçoise garnish and just serving with a green salad.

❶ Cook all the potatoes, including those for the Niçoise garnish, in boiling salted water for 10–12 minutes or until tender. Drain, then remove the slices. Return the diced potatoes to the pan to dry out.

❷ Fry the onion in olive oil for a few minutes until golden brown, then add the chilli and mixed herbs and cook for 5 minutes, until softened.

❸ Prepare the Niçoise garnish.

❹ Make the potato cakes: mix together the onion mixture, the olives, basil and chopped tomatoes. Add the diced potatoes and crush with a fork. Stir in the egg yolk and season generously. Divide the mixture into six balls. Roll in the seasoned flour and flatten gently.

❺ Heat a large frying pan and add 2 tablespoons of oil. Fry the potato cakes for 2–3 minutes until golden and heated through.

❻ Arrange the Niçoise garnish and potato cakes on serving plates, and drizzle with the dressing.

...the niçoise garnish

1 potato, cut into four thick slices
Olive oil, for char-grilling
1 red pepper, quartered and seeded
100 g (4 oz) French beans, trimmed
2 small vine-ripened tomatoes
2 eggs
25 ml (1 fl oz) balsamic vinegar
50 ml (2 fl oz) extra virgin olive oil
1 tablespoon freshly grated Parmesan
Salt and freshly ground black pepper

❶ Cook the potato in boiling salted water for 10-12 minutes. (You can save time by cooking the potatoes for both the potato cakes and the Niçoise garnish together.)

❷ Brush a griddle pan with oil and heat until smoking hot. Arrange the pepper quarters in the pan with the potato slices and cook until lightly charred, turning occasionally.

❸ Blanch the beans in a pan of boiling salted water, then drain. Cut a cross in the bottom of the two tomatoes, blanch briefly, then skin them, leaving the stalks intact.

❹ Cook the eggs in a small pan of water for 4½ minutes or until hard-boiled, depending on how you like them. Drain and refresh under cold running water, shell and halve.

❺ Just before serving, make the dressing: mix together the balsamic vinegar, extra virgin olive oil and grated Parmesan and season with plenty of pepper.

hot tips

● Do not cook your eggs for more than 12 minutes or a black ring will form around the yolks. Placing them under cold running water stops them from cooking further.

● When buying tomatoes use your nose. If they smell like tomatoes there's every chance they'll taste like them.

bombay curried potatoes with peas by patrick anthony

2 large baking potatoes, cut into cubes

2 tablespoons sunflower oil

I onion, halved and sliced

I red or yellow pepper, seeded and diced

2–3 teaspoons medium curry powder

2 teaspoons coriander seeds,
crushed to a powder

2 garlic cloves, finely chopped

Juice of ½ lemon

85 ml (3 fl oz) hot water

75 g (3 oz) frozen peas

2 tablespoons Greek yoghurt (optional)

2 tablespoons roughly chopped
fresh coriander, to garnish

Salt and freshly ground black pepper

Naan bread, to serve (optional)

This simple dish is prepared with traditional curry spices and shows how a few humble ingredients can be transformed into a quick and delicious supper.

❶ Place the potatoes in a pan of boiling salted water, bring back to the boil and simmer for 5 minutes, then drain well.

❷ Meanwhile, heat a wok or large frying pan and add the oil. Tip in the onion and pepper and cook gently for 5 minutes or until softened. Add the curry powder, coriander seeds and garlic and stir-fry for 20 seconds. Add the blanched potatoes and toss until well coated in the spices.

❸ Stir the lemon juice and ½ teaspoon of salt into the hot water and mix well to combine. Pour into the wok or frying pan, cover and simmer, stirring occasionally, for 8–10 minutes, or until most of the liquid has evaporated and the potatoes are tender when pierced with a knife.

❹ Add the peas, stir in and cook for 2–3 minutes until they are tender but still bright green. Season to taste.

❺ Spoon the potatoes on to each serving plate and add a dollop of yoghurt, if using. Scatter over the coriander and serve with naan bread, if liked.

hot tip

● To make easy work of seeding a pepper, cut off the top, turn it upside down and slice off the cheeks all round leaving just the membrane and seeds to be thrown away. Slice as needed.

above: **potato cakes with a niçoise garnish (page 30-31)**

below: **sweetcorn and sweet potato chowder (page 15)**

above: **open mushroom lasagne (page 26)**

below: **stir-fried seafood with chinese black beans and noodles (page 38)**

above: **honey-roast quail on polenta with grape salsa (page 61)**

below: **barbecued lamb with french bean salad and tzatziki (84)**

above: **floating cheese soufflés (page 16)**

below: **mackerel brochettes with warm spicy potato salad (page 46-47)**

above: **fiery cocktail sausages with onion marmalade (page 82)**

above: **mexican salsa pizza (page 50)**

below: **aromatic lamb and spinach balti (page 79) with chapatis (page 80)**

above: **paprika seared chicken on a broccoli stir-fry (page 64)**

above: **apricot tarte tatin with walnut cream (page 92)**

below: **hot strawberry and raspberry pavlovas (page 89)**

chana dal

by patrick anthony

25 g (1 oz) unsalted butter
2 tablespoons sunflower oil
3 garlic cloves
1 onion, finely chopped
2 teaspoons grated fresh root ginger
½ teaspoon salt
1 teaspoon ground turmeric
2 green chillies, seeded and finely chopped
400g (14 oz) can pease pudding
175 ml (6 fl oz) hot water

A gastronomic breakthrough! This usually takes at least 1½ hours to cook but this inspired substitute using canned pease pudding means you can literally make it in minutes!

❶ Heat the butter and half the oil in a wok or frying pan. Finely chop 2 garlic cloves and add to the pan with the onion and ginger. Cook for a few minutes until the onion is softened.
❷ Stir in the salt and turmeric, then add the chillies, pease pudding and hot water. Mix well and bring to the boil, then reduce the heat and simmer gently for 5 minutes, stirring occasionally, until slightly thickened.
❸ Meanwhile, heat the remaining oil in a small pan. Thinly slice the remaining garlic clove and add to the pan. Cook for a minute or so until golden brown.
❹ Tip the chana dal into a warmed serving bowl and drizzle over the garlic oil. Serve at once.

prawn kedgeree   35

spaghetti with orecchiette sauce   36

salmon and ginger baklava pie   37

stir-fried seafood with chinese black beans

   and noodles   38

smoked haddock fish cakes with red onion salsa   39

cod fish pie   40

thai green curry with prawns and jasmine rice   41

seared salmon with savoury lentils   42

baked mackerel with lemon, soy and mushrooms   44

blackened salmon with cucumber salad   45

mackerel brochettes with warm spicy potato salad   46

prawn kedgeree

by nick nairn

100 g (4 oz) unsalted butter
1 small onion, finely chopped
½ teaspoon ground turmeric
1 teaspoon curry powder
1 green chilli, seeded and finely chopped
2.5 cm (1 in) piece fresh root ginger,
peeled and finely chopped
300 g (10 oz) cooked long-grain rice
225 g (8 oz) cooked peeled prawns,
thawed if frozen
2 hard-boiled eggs, shelled and quartered
1 teaspoon cayenne pepper
Maldon salt and freshly ground
black pepper
1 tablespoon chopped fresh parsley,
to garnish

This is an adaptation of a classic dish. It's great for Sunday brunch or a light evening meal.

❶ Melt the butter in a large frying pan. Add the onion and cook over a low heat until softened. Add the turmeric, curry powder, chilli and ginger to the pan and cook for 1–2 minutes. ❷ Add the rice, prawns and egg quarters to the pan. Stir over a high heat until heated through. Sprinkle in the cayenne and season with salt and pepper. Pile the kedgeree on to two serving plates and garnish with chopped parsley.

hot tip

● When you have cooked the rice for this dish, spread it out on a tray to cool. This will stop the grains sticking together.

spaghetti with orecchiette sauce

by ross burden

200 g (7 oz) head of broccoli, cut into
florets, the stem peeled and thinly sliced
175 g (6 oz) dried spaghetti
3 canned anchovy fillets, drained
3 tablespoons olive oil
1 large garlic clove, thinly sliced
1 long red chilli, seeded and cut into rings
Salt and freshly ground black pepper
Freshly grated Parmesan, to garnish

hot tip

● The term *al dente* means that the pasta is tender but still slightly firm to the bite and not soft. To find out if the spaghetti is cooked, remove a small piece and taste it. Drain immediately to stop it cooking further.

Avoid any spaghetti that lists 'disodium phosphate' on the label. It is a chemical softening agent that helps pasta cook faster but it also reduces the flavour. Use good-quality dried pasta for the best results and always cook it *al dente*.

❶ Bring two large pans of salted water to the boil. Place the broccoli in one pan and cook for 5–6 minutes, or until just tender, then drain and refresh under cold running water. Drop the spaghetti into the other pan, adding a large pinch of salt, and cook for 8–10 minutes or according to packet instructions, until *al dente*.

❷ Place the anchovies in a large frying pan with the oil. Cook over a low heat until the anchovies begin to 'melt'. Add the garlic and chilli and cook for a further 2 minutes. Add the broccoli to the pan and increase the heat. Cook for 1–2 minutes or until just heated through.

❸ Drain the pasta, return to the pan, add the broccoli mixture and toss well to combine. Divide between two warmed wide-rimmed serving bowls, grind black pepper on top and garnish with grated Parmesan to serve.

salmon and ginger baklava pie

by lesley waters

150 g (5 oz) packet 23 x 30 cm
(9 x 12 in) filo pastry sheets,
thawed if frozen
50 g (2 oz) melted butter
15 g (½ oz) natural dried breadcrumbs
175 g (6 oz) small broccoli florets
450 g (1 lb) skinless salmon fillet,
cut into large dice
1 teaspoon grated fresh root ginger
1 red chilli, seeded and finely chopped
Finely grated rind and juice of ½ lemon
175 g (6 oz) Greek yoghurt
1 egg, beaten
5 tablespoons grapeseed oil
1 teaspoon clear honey
Few drops of Tabasco sauce
2 tablespoons roughly chopped
fresh coriander
Salt and freshly ground black pepper

This sophisticated fish pie looks impressive but is incredibly simple and quick to make. To balance the rich flavours, I serve it with a crisp green salad.

❶ Pre-heat the oven to gas mark 6, 200°C (400°F). Place a sheet of filo pastry on a large, non-stick baking sheet and brush with a little melted butter. Layer up three more sheets, brushing with butter as you go, then sprinkle with the breadcrumbs.

❷ Plunge the broccoli florets into a pan of boiling salted water and cook for 2–3 minutes until just tender. Drain and refresh under cold running water, then arrange on top of the breadcrumbs.

❸ In a large bowl, mix together the salmon, ginger, chilli, lemon rind, yoghurt, egg and seasoning. Spoon the mixture over the broccoli florets. Place a sheet of filo on top and press down gently to seal. Brush with melted butter and continue to layer in the same way until all the pastry is used up. Score the top layer of the pastry in a criss-cross pattern and trim the edges, using a sharp knife. Bake for 15–20 minutes until the salmon is tender and the pastry is golden.

❹ Place the oil, lemon juice and honey in a small pan. Season and add Tabasco to taste. Heat gently, then remove from the heat and stir in the coriander. Remove the pie from the oven, pour over the warm dressing, then cut into slices to serve.

stir-fried seafood with chinese black beans and noodles by paul rankin

250 g (9 oz) medium egg noodles

2 tablespoons sunflower oil

1 small red onion, sliced

1 red pepper, seeded and sliced

1 garlic clove, finely chopped

1 green chilli, seeded and finely sliced

300 g (10 oz) packet mixed fresh seafood
(such as prawns, squid, mussels)

4 spring onions, cut into
4 cm (1½ in) slices

1 teaspoon cornflour

2–3 tablespoons black bean sauce
from a jar

2 tablespoons dry sherry

1 teaspoon sugar

85 ml (3 fl oz) warm water

1 tablespoon sesame oil

1 dessertspoon light soy sauce

1 tablespoon roughly chopped fresh
coriander, to garnish

I'm a real noodle fan and this dish is packed with flavour and texture – be warned, everyone will want second helpings.

❶ Bring a large pan of salted water to the boil. Add the egg noodles and cook for 4 minutes or according to packet instructions. Tip into a sieve and leave to drain well.

❷ Heat the oil in a large wok or frying pan. When very hot, add the red onion and pepper slices and garlic and stir-fry for 1–2 minutes. Add the chilli, mixed seafood and spring onions to the pan and cook, tossing from time to time, over a very high heat for about 2 minutes or until the seafood is just tender and almost golden.

❸ Place the cornflour in a small jug and add the black bean sauce, sherry, sugar and warm water. Beat until well combined. Add to the wok or pan and cook for 1–2 minutes until thickened slightly.

❹ Heat another wok or heavy-based frying pan until very hot. Toss the noodles with the sesame oil and soy sauce. Place in the pan and cook for a few minutes until just beginning to crisp on the bottom. Divide the noodles between two serving plates, arrange the seafood mixture on top and garnish with coriander.

hot tips

● As a general rule, the smaller the chilli the hotter it will be.

● Fresh seafood should always smell of the sea and should be bright and moist.

smoked haddock fish cakes with red onion salsa by nick nairn

350 g (12 oz) floury potatoes, such as
Romano, cut into chunks
25 g (1 oz) unsalted butter
450 g (1 lb) undyed skinless smoked
haddock fillet
300 ml (10 fl oz) milk
2 tablespoons chopped fresh parsley
Sunflower oil, for deep-frying
25 g (1 oz) plain flour, seasoned with salt
and pepper, plus extra for dusting
75 g (3 oz) fresh white breadcrumbs
2 eggs, beaten

FOR THE RED ONION SALSA
1 small red onion, finely chopped
2 small ripe tomatoes, peeled and diced
1 large garlic clove, crushed
1 long red chilli, seeded and finely diced
Juice of 1 lime
100 ml (3½ fl oz) extra virgin olive oil
Handful of chopped fresh coriander leaves

Maldon salt and freshly ground
black pepper
Handful of fresh coriander leaves,
to garnish

I love cooking with smoked haddock – it has a delicious flavour and flakes into good, firm chunks that are perfect for this dish.

❶ Boil the potatoes until tender, then drain or, to save time, place the potatoes in a microwave-proof dish with 150 ml (5 fl oz) of boiling water. Cook on high for 8 minutes or until tender. Drain well, mash with the butter and cool slightly.

❷ Place the fish, milk and a little seasoning in a small pan and poach the fish for 2–3 minutes. Remove with a slotted spoon and reserve the milk. Flake the fish into small pieces, discarding any bones.

❸ Add the fish, parsley and 2 tablespoons of the reserved milk to the potatoes, season and mix well. Divide the mixture into eight and shape into patties, dusting with flour if necessary. Place on a baking tray, cover and, ideally, chill in the refrigerator for 20 minutes, or place in the freezer for 5 minutes.

❹ Make the red onion salsa: place the onion, tomatoes and garlic in a bowl with the chilli, lime juice and olive oil. Season and add the coriander, mix well and leave at room temperature.

❺ Heat about 5 cm (2 in) of oil in a large heavy-based pan. Place the seasoned flour on a shallow plate, the breadcrumbs in a shallow dish and the beaten eggs in a shallow bowl. Lightly dust the fish cakes in the flour, then dip them in the egg and finally coat with the breadcrumbs. Fry for 2–3 minutes on each side or until lightly golden and heated through. Drain well on kitchen paper. Place the coriander leaves in the centre of the plate, top with a fish cake and drizzle round the salsa.

cod fish pie

by paul rankin

25 g (1 oz) unsalted butter

1 leek, thinly sliced

75 g (3 oz) button mushrooms, sliced

225 g (8 oz) large potato, sliced

4 eggs

150 ml (5 fl oz) milk

3 tablespoons chopped fresh dill

300 g (10 oz) skinless boneless cod fillet,
cut into 2 cm (¾ in) cubes

50 g (2 oz) Cheddar, grated

120 ml (4 fl oz) double cream

2 tablespoons wholegrain mustard

Salt and freshly ground black pepper

Fresh dill sprigs, to garnish

hot tips

● If you don't like leeks or haven't got any, substitute a thinly sliced onion, spring onions or even celery. And instead of mushrooms you could use a red pepper or broccoli florets.

● The pie can be prepared in advance. Scatter the fish over the cooked potato, pour over the beaten egg mixture, cover and chill. For a special treat, cover the pie with puff pastry before chilling. Pop it into the hot oven when you are ready.

This is my own version of one of my favourite childhood dishes which I still make when I have a craving for comfort food.

❶ Pre-heat the oven to gas mark 7, 220°C (425°F). Take a rectangular 5 cm (2 in) deep, microwave- and ovenproof-dish and heat it gently over a low heat. Place the butter, leek slices and mushrooms in the dish, then add the potato in an even layer. Season generously and add a splash of water. Cover with non-PVC plastic film and pierce a couple of times with a knife. Microwave on high for 5 minutes or until the potatoes are almost tender.

If you don't have a microwave, melt the butter in a pan. Add the leeks and fry until softened, then add the mushrooms and cook for a further minute. Transfer to an ovenproof dish. Cook the potatoes in a pan of boiling salted water for 8–10 minutes until just tender, then layer over the leeks and mushrooms.

❷ Place the eggs and milk in a jug and beat until combined, then add 2 tablespoons of dill and season generously.

❸ Scatter the fish on top of the potato layer, season with salt and pour over the egg mixture, stirring slightly. Place in the oven for 5 minutes. Remove from the oven, sprinkle over the cheese, then return to the oven for 8–10 minutes. To finish, pre-heat the grill to hot and place the dish underneath until the cheese is bubbling and golden.

❹ Reduce the cream in a pan until slightly thickened, stir in the mustard and remaining dill and season. Divide the pie between two warmed plates, spoon over the sauce and garnish.

thai green curry with prawns and jasmine rice by patrick anthony

175 g (6 oz) jasmine rice, well rinsed
½ teaspoon salt
1 tablespoon sunflower oil
2 heaped tablespoons finely chopped onion
2 teaspoons grated fresh root ginger
1 tablespoon Thai fish sauce (nam pla)
3–4 teaspoons Thai green curry paste
225 ml (8 fl oz) hot water
50 g (2 oz) grated creamed coconut from a block
225 g (8 oz) peeled raw tiger or king prawns, thawed if frozen
1 green chilli, seeded and finely chopped
Handful of fresh coriander leaves
Lime wedges, to garnish

Swift, but simple and with all the taste thrills of Thailand. I like to serve this with jasmine rice which has its own delicate fragrance.

❶ Place the rice in a pan with 350 ml (12 fl oz) of water and the salt and bring to the boil. Stir once, then reduce the heat to its lowest setting, cover and cook for 8–10 minutes. Remove the pan from the heat and leave, covered and undisturbed, for 5 minutes.

❷ Heat the oil in a wok or large frying pan. Add the onion and cook for 1–2 minutes or until softened. Add the ginger, fish sauce, curry paste, hot water and grated coconut. Heat, stirring, until just below boiling point, then add the prawns and cook gently for 3–4 minutes until the prawns are tender and just cooked through.

❸ Fluff up the rice grains with a fork and divide between the serving plates. Spoon on the curry and scatter over the chilli and the coriander leaves. Garnish with lime wedges to serve.

hot tip

● Thai fish sauce is made from fermented salted anchovies and brings an added lift to any Thai dish. Galangal is among the many ingredients in the Thai green curry paste, which will keep in the fridge for 3–4 weeks after opening. A root-like stem or rhizome, galangal is related to ginger and tastes quite similar. Great in curries, it is available fresh, dried and ground.

seared salmon with savoury lentils

by nick nairn

1 tablespoon sunflower oil
150 g (5 oz) skinless salmon fillet, cut in
half lengthways
1 tablespoon fresh lime juice
Maldon salt and freshly ground
black pepper
Handful of fresh parsley and coriander
leaves, to garnish

hot tip

● To store fresh parsley, wash the sprigs and pat them dry. Place in a polythene bag, tied very loosely, and store in the bottom of the fridge for a few days.

The golden rule when cooking salmon for a recipe like this is to veer towards slightly undercooking, to ensure that it stays moist and tender.

❶ Make the savoury lentils.

❷ Heat the oil in a frying pan until very hot, season the salmon all over and add to the pan. Fry for 1–2 minutes each side, or until lightly golden. Sprinkle over the lime juice and rest on a warmed plate for a couple of minutes.

❸ Divide the lentils between two warmed serving plates, arrange the fish on top and garnish with the parsley and coriander.

...the savoury lentils

25 ml (1 fl oz) olive oil
1 carrot, finely chopped
2 celery sticks, finely chopped
1 small leek, finely chopped
2.5 cm (1 in) piece fresh root ginger,
peeled and finely chopped
1 garlic clove, finely chopped
1 teaspoon mild curry powder
400 g (14 oz) can Puy lentils, drained
150 ml (5 fl oz) fish or chicken stock
2 small tomatoes,
peeled, quartered and finely chopped
2 tablespoons Greek yoghurt
1 tablespoon chopped fresh
flatleaf parsley
Maldon salt and freshly ground black
pepper

❶ Heat the olive oil in a heavy-based pan, then add the carrot, celery, leek, ginger and garlic. Cook for a couple of minutes until softened, then stir in the curry powder, season and cook for 2 minutes until just beginning to colour.

❷ Stir in the lentils, add the stock and bring to the boil. Reduce the heat, add the tomatoes, season and simmer gently for 5–6 minutes.

❸ Just before serving, add the yoghurt and chopped parsley to the lentils, stir and heat through.

hot tip

● Canned lentils are a fantastic store-cupboard stand-by and for once taste almost as good as the real thing. Puy lentils are smaller, finer and have a better flavour than other lentils, but if you can't find them use brown or green ones.

baked mackerel with lemon, soy and mushrooms by paul rankin

2 fresh mackerel, filleted with skin left on
50 g (2 oz) unsalted butter
150 g (5 oz) shiitake or brown cap mushrooms, sliced
4 thin lemon slices
1 tablespoon fresh lemon juice
2 tablespoons light soy sauce
Freshly ground black pepper

This is a great way to jazz up mackerel. The relatively strong flavour of the fish stands up well to the oriental ingredients.

❶ Pre-heat the oven to gas mark 7, 220°C (425°F). Cut each mackerel fillet in half, widthways, on a slight angle. Spread a little of the butter on to two 30 cm (12 in) foil squares. In the centre of each square, place four mackerel pieces, skin-side up.
❷ Scatter the mushrooms over the fish, then divide the lemon slices, lemon juice and soy sauce between the parcels and dot with the remaining butter. Season generously with pepper. Gather up the foil edges, crimping them together to ensure the package is tightly sealed.
❸ Bake for 10–15 minutes until the fish is just cooked. Place an unopened package on each plate and allow each person to open theirs and release the steamy aromas of the mackerel.

hot tip

● Always choose mushrooms that are firm-textured, with fresh-looking stalks that are not withered. Use mushrooms as soon as possible after buying as they do not keep well.

blackened salmon with cucumber salad by nick nairn

1 dessertspoon paprika
½ teaspoon dried thyme
½ teaspoon dried oregano
½ teaspoon black peppercorns, crushed
½ teaspoon cumin seeds
2 x 175 g (6 oz) thick salmon fillet pieces, scaled
2 tablespoons olive oil
1 small cucumber, peeled, halved and seeded
1 large garlic clove, crushed
1 dessertspoon fresh lime juice
1 red finger chilli, seeded and finely chopped
1 tablespoon chopped fresh coriander
Salt and freshly ground pepper

My absolute favourite way to eat salmon is when it's quickly seared in a hot pan. It's one of my signature dishes and for a light, summer supper I like to serve it with a fresh, crisp cucumber salad.

❶ Mix together the paprika, thyme, oregano, peppercorns and cumin seeds on a plate. Score the salmon flesh in a criss-cross fashion and brush all over with a little of the oil. Dip the pieces, skin-side down, into the spice mixture ensuring they are well coated.

❷ Grate the cucumber into long, thin shreds. Salt well and leave to drain in a sieve set over a bowl.

❸ Heat a griddle pan until smoking hot and brush with a little olive oil. Fry the salmon pieces, skin side down, for 3–4 minutes until the skin starts to crisp, then turn them over and cook for 2–3 minutes or until the salmon is just cooked through. Rest for a couple of minutes before serving.

❹ Rinse the cucumber, squeeze it dry in a clean tea towel and place in a bowl. Add the garlic, lime juice, chilli and coriander, season generously and mix well to combine. Place a mound of cucumber salad on the centre of each serving plate and arrange the salmon to the side. Serve at once.

mackerel brochettes with warm spicy potato salad by nick nairn

I red chilli, finely chopped

Grated rind of I lemon

2 tablespoons olive oil

I garlic clove, crushed

I large mackerel, cleaned, filleted and cut into 2.5 cm (I in) pieces

I tablespoon fresh lemon juice

Salt and freshly ground black pepper

Chopped fresh flatleaf parsley, to garnish

Lemon or lime wedges, to serve

hot tip

● Oily fish are ideal for barbecuing as they don't dry out. If you don't fancy mackerel, try salmon or tuna.

If you're looking to eat healthily, you really can't beat fresh mackerel. It is available all year round and is very economical so, accompanied as here with a delicious potato salad, it makes the perfect meal.

❶ Pre-heat the barbecue, if using.

❷ In a bowl, mix together the chilli, lemon rind, olive oil, garlic and salt and pepper. Add the fish pieces and ensure they are well coated. Marinate for at least 5 minutes, or a maximum of 15 minutes, then add the lemon juice.

❸ Make the warm spicy potato salad.

❹ Thread the pieces of fish on to metal skewers (if you are using wooden skewers soak them in water for 30 minutes to stop them burning). Place the fish on the barbecue or heat a griddle pan until hot. Cook for 2–3 minutes on each side, turning and basting frequently with the marinade until the fish pieces are nicely marked and just tender.

❺ Pile the potatoes on to two serving plates and place the fish brochettes on top. Garnish with chopped fresh flatleaf parsley and serve with lemon or lime wedges.

...the warm spicy potato salad

250 g (9 oz) baby new potatoes, sliced

2 tablespoons sunflower oil

¼ teaspoon cayenne pepper

¼ teaspoon ground turmeric

¼ teaspoon garam masala

¼ teaspoon lightly crushed coriander seeds

2 tablespoons chopped fresh
flatleaf parsley

Pinch of salt

❶ Cook the potato slices for 7–8 minutes in boiling salted water to par-boil them, then drain.

❷ Heat the sunflower oil in a frying pan, add the potato slices and cook for 3–4 minutes, tossing occasionally. Add the cayenne pepper, turmeric, garam masala and coriander seeds and cook for 2–3 minutes, turning frequently, until the potatoes are coated in a rich spicy crust.

❸ Just before serving, stir in the parsley.

hot tips

● The flavours in the potato salad improve if it is made in advance. Reheat in the frying pan on the side of the barbecue, in the oven, or even in the microwave while the fish is cooking.

● A disposable barbecue is great when you are cooking for just two people. Light it about 35 minutes before you want to cook and wait until a layer of grey ash appears and there is an even heat when you pass your hand above the coals.

tandoori chicken skewers with cucumber salad by richard cawley

2 garlic cloves, crushed

½ teaspoon minced ginger from a jar

2 teaspoons medium tandoori paste

3 tablespoons Greek yoghurt

I lemon

225 g (8 oz) skinless, boneless chicken breast fillet, cut into 2.5 cm (I in) cubes

½ cucumber, halved lengthways, seeded and thinly sliced

I red chilli, seeded and finely chopped

Handful of fresh basil, roughly torn

Pinch of paprika

Pinch of salt

2 tablespoons mango chutney, to glaze

Lemon wedges and chapatis (see page 80) or naan bread, to serve (optional)

I love this type of light Indian food. The tandoori chicken skewers contrast beautifully in both flavour and texture with the fresh, crispy cucumber salad.

❶ Mix together the garlic, ginger, tandoori paste and yoghurt in a non-metallic bowl. Add a good squeeze of lemon juice, then stir in the chicken and marinate for at least 5 minutes or up to 24 hours covered in the fridge.

❷ Meanwhile, make the cucumber salad: place the cucumber, chilli and basil in a bowl. Squeeze over the remaining lemon juice and stir in the paprika and a little salt, to taste. Toss well to combine.

❸ Pre-heat the grill to high. Arrange the chicken on four 15 cm (6 in) bamboo skewers, soaked in water for at least 30 minutes to prevent them burning, and grill for 2–3 minutes on each side until just tender. Brush with a little mango chutney and serve hot with the cucumber salad, lemon wedges, and chapatis or naan bread if liked.

hot tip

● The longer you marinate the chicken pieces the more tandoori flavour they will have. If you are using metal skewers, try to find the flat ones. These will stop the chicken pieces rolling round while you are turning them.

mexican salsa pizza

by lesley waters

4 tablespoons extra virgin olive oil

1 garlic clove

1 mild red chilli, lightly scored

2 x 125 g (4½ oz) packets or
1 x 290 g (11 oz) packet pizza base mix

½ lemon

1 teaspoon ground cumin

2 x 100 g (4 oz) turkey breast fillets,
flattened out thinly and sliced

1 red onion, sliced

400 g (14 oz) can chopped tomatoes in
rich tomato sauce,
drained and juice reserved

1 red pepper, seeded and
roughly chopped

Pinch of sugar

1 teaspoon Tabasco sauce

100 g (4 oz) cherry tomatoes, quartered

100 g (4 oz) baby sweetcorn

2 tablespoons Greek yoghurt or
soured cream

2 tablespoons roughly chopped
fresh coriander

Salt and freshly ground black pepper

In the time it takes to ring and have a take-away pizza delivered, you could be enjoying this spicy dish.

❶ Pre-heat the oven to gas mark 6, 200°C (400°F). Place 2 tablespoons of oil in a pan with the garlic and chilli. Heat gently for 1 minute, then remove from the heat and set aside.

❷ Make the pizza dough according to packet instructions and roll out into a 30 cm (12 in) circle. Place on a baking sheet (or a large paella pan, if you have one), brush with 1 tablespoon of oil and bake for 10–12 minutes until golden.

❸ Place the remaining oil in a non-metallic dish. Squeeze in the lemon juice and add the cumin. Season to taste and mix to combine. Stir in the turkey and onion and marinate for at least 5 minutes or up to 24 hours covered in the fridge.

❹ Remove the garlic and chilli from the oil and discard, then pour the oil into a food processor and add the chopped tomatoes, red pepper, sugar and Tabasco. Whizz briefly, then tip into a bowl, season and add the cherry tomatoes. Stir in a little of the reserved tomato juice if the salsa is too thick.

❺ Heat a large frying pan. Add the turkey and onion mixture and stir-fry for 4–5 minutes or until the turkey is cooked. Plunge the sweetcorn into simmering water and cook for 4–5 minutes until just tender. Drain and refresh under cold running water.

❻ Spread the tomato salsa over the pizza base and pile the turkey and sweetcorn on top. Spoon over teaspoons of the yoghurt or soured cream and scatter with coriander, then cut into wedges to serve.

chicken tikka platter

by lesley waters

4 skinless, boneless chicken thighs,
well trimmed and cut into strips
2 heaped tablespoons tikka masala
curry paste
Sunflower oil, for frying
225 g (8 oz) French beans, trimmed
100 g (4 oz) tender young spinach leaves
Salt and freshly ground black pepper

FOR THE INDIAN LATKES
Sunflower oil, for frying
1 large potato, grated and squeezed dry
1 egg
1 heaped tablespoon plain flour
½ teaspoon baking powder
1 heaped teaspoon garam masala

hot tips

● As well as adding to the taste, the marinade stops the chicken drying out during cooking.
● Latkes are an Eastern European dish. They should be shaped and cooked immediately after mixing in the baking powder. They freeze well after cooking. Reheat, covered, in an oven pre-heated to gas mark 5, 190°C (375°F).

This may not be an authentic Indian-style tikka that takes days to make but, nonetheless, the results are very tasty.

❶ Place the chicken in a shallow dish and mix with the tikka masala paste. Leave to marinate for at least 5 minutes or up to 24 hours covered in the fridge.
❷ Make the latkes: cover the base of a large frying pan with a film of oil and heat. Mix the dry grated potato with the egg, flour, baking powder and garam masala. Divide the mixture into six mounds and cook the latkes for 3–4 minutes on each side until golden. Drain on kitchen paper.
❸ Heat a wok or large frying pan until hot, add a little oil and stir-fry the chicken and its marinade for 5–7 minutes until the chicken is tender. Season to taste with plenty of black pepper and keep warm.
❹ Blanch the beans in boiling salted water for 2 minutes until just tender, then drain and refresh under cold running water. Heat a little oil in the wok until hot, then toss in the beans and cook for a few minutes. Toss in the spinach, stirring to coat. Season to taste and cook for 1 minute or until the spinach leaves begin to wilt.
❺ Arrange the bean mixture on a serving plate. Spoon over some of the chicken mixture and serve with the latkes.

cheat's coq au vin

by kevin woodford

2 tablespoons olive oil

6 skinless, boneless chicken thighs, trimmed of fat

4 rashers streaky bacon, cut widthways into thin strips

100 g (4 oz) small button onions

1 garlic clove, crushed

300 ml (10 fl oz) red wine

1 tablespoon tomato purée

1 teaspoon fresh thyme leaves

1 bay leaf

1 tablespoon plain flour

1 tablespoon softened unsalted butter

Salt and freshly ground black pepper

1 tablespoon chopped fresh flatleaf parsley, to garnish

For a rich, tasty and succulent meal, look no further – the depth of flavour in this dish is fantastic, especially when you consider that it takes less than 20 minutes to prepare.

❶ Heat the oil in a frying pan. Add the chicken and fry for 4 minutes, turning once, until golden. Add the bacon and onions and cook for a few minutes.

❷ Add the garlic, pour in the wine, then add the tomato purée, thyme leaves and bay leaf. Season to taste. Bring to a simmer and cook for 8–10 minutes until the chicken is tender, stirring occasionally.

❸ Mix the flour and butter to make a smooth paste. Add a couple of tablespoons of the cooking liquid and mix again until smooth. Stir the paste into the pan and simmer for a few minutes until the sauce has thickened, then season to taste and sprinkle with parsley to serve.

rabbit with apricot and orange

by patrick anthony

350 g (12 oz) rabbit loin fillet, sliced or
450 g (1 lb) boneless rabbit pieces
1 garlic clove, crushed
1 tablespoon sunflower oil
15 g (½ oz) unsalted butter
Grated rind and juice of 1 orange –
about 50 ml (2 fl oz)
50 ml (2 fl oz) dry white wine
100 ml (3½ fl oz) chicken stock
25 g (1 oz) ready-to-eat apricots,
finely chopped
1 teaspoon light muscovado sugar
1½ teaspoons white-wine vinegar
1 teaspoon cornflour or
arrowroot (optional)
Salt and freshly ground black pepper
1 teaspoon dark soy sauce, to serve

The rabbit in this dish is simmered in a sensational apricot and orange sauce surrounded with a contrasting 'necklace' of dark soy sauce droplets. I like to eat it with boiled new potatoes, but fragrant jasmine rice would also work well.

❶ Heat a frying pan. Season the rabbit pieces generously and rub all over with the garlic. Add the oil and butter to the pan and once the butter is sizzling, fry the rabbit pieces for 2–3 minutes on each side until lightly browned.

❷ Place the orange rind and juice, the wine and stock in a jug with the apricots and stir to combine. Spoon off any excess oil from the pan and pour in the orange juice mixture. Bring to the boil, then reduce the heat and simmer gently for 5–6 minutes until the liquid is slightly reduced.

❸ Add the sugar and vinegar to the pan and continue to cook for 1–2 minutes or until the rabbit is tender. If you would like the sauce a bit thicker mix the cornflour or arrowroot with a little water, add to the pan and simmer gently for 1–2 minutes. Arrange the rabbit pieces on serving plates and spoon over the sauce. Sprinkle droplets of soy sauce around the edges of the plates to serve.

sesame chicken sauté

by lesley waters

3 tablespoons wholegrain mustard

I tablespoon clear honey

Juice of I lemon

I tablespoon sesame oil

2 skinless, boneless chicken breast fillets, sliced into thin strips

2 teaspoons olive oil

I tablespoon sesame seeds

I ripe avocado, peeled, stoned and sliced

75 g (3 oz) packet mixed salad leaves

FOR THE VINAIGRETTE

2 teaspoons white-wine vinegar

Pinch of sugar

3 tablespoons sunflower oil

Salt and freshly ground black pepper

I think it is fair to say that this is my all-time favourite stand-by supper dish. It literally takes minutes to prepare and not much longer to eat.

❶ Place the mustard, honey, lemon juice and sesame oil in a shallow non-metallic dish and mix well. Add the chicken strips, stir to coat and season to taste.

❷ Heat the olive oil in a wok until very hot, tip in the chicken mixture and stir-fry for 5–6 minutes or until the chicken strips are tender and lightly caramelized. Heat a small pan and dry-fry the sesame seeds until lightly golden, stirring occasionally.

❸ Meanwhile, make the vinaigrette: place the vinegar in a small bowl with the sugar and plenty of seasoning. Whisk until everything is dissolved, then whisk in the oil.

❹ Toss the avocado with the salad leaves and vinaigrette and pile on to serving plates. Sprinkle with the sesame seeds and scatter the chicken on top to serve.

french-style venison with
mushrooms by patrick anthony

4 x 50 g (2 oz) venison escalopes
I dessertspoon sunflower oil
15 g (½ oz) unsalted butter
I teaspoon plain flour
I heaped teaspoon Dijon mustard
I small garlic clove, crushed
150 ml (5 fl oz) dry cider
2 teaspoons redcurrant jelly
75 g (3 oz) button mushrooms, sliced
4 tablespoons soured cream
Salt and freshly ground black pepper
Chopped fresh flatleaf parsley, to garnish

hot tip

● If you can't get hold of redcurrant jelly, or want to try something different, substitute it with rowan jelly which is a traditional accompaniment to game. Cranberry jelly would also work well.

This is really incredibly easy and you only need one large frying pan. To make it extra-special, serve with a delicious root vegetable purée. Mash equal quantities of cooked parsnip and potato together with a knob of butter and a splash of milk.

❶ Heat a large frying pan. Season the venison all over. Add the oil and butter to the pan and once the butter is sizzling, fry the venison escalopes for 1–2 minutes on each side until lightly browned and just tender. Transfer to a plate and keep warm.

❷ Add the flour, mustard and garlic to the pan and stir briskly until combined. Gradually pour in the cider, stirring continuously, and bring to the boil. Season generously, stir in the redcurrant jelly and cook for 1–2 minutes, stirring, until the jelly has melted.

❸ Stir in the mushrooms and simmer for 2–3 minutes, then stir in the soured cream and bring back to a simmer. Season to taste. Arrange the venison on serving plates, spoon over the sauce and sprinkle with parsley to garnish before serving.

herbed chicken en croûte

by kevin woodford

Olive oil, for frying
2 boneless chicken breast fillets, skin on
2 tablespoons Dijon mustard
Bunch of mixed fresh herbs
(such as tarragon, parsley, mint and basil),
finely chopped
1 x 375 g (13 oz) packet ready-rolled puff
pastry, thawed if frozen
Beaten egg, to glaze
1 small swede, cubed
2 large carrots, sliced
1 large onion, sliced
150 ml (5 fl oz) dry white wine
1 tablespoon chicken stock
50 g (2 oz) unsalted butter, diced
Salt and freshly ground black pepper

hot tips

● Chicken en croûte is a perfect dinner party dish and can be made the day before. Keep it covered in the fridge, then just pop it into the oven while you are having a drink.

● I've left the skin on the breast as the thin layer of fat below it protects the flesh during cooking and keeps it moist.

Swede and carrots are a perfect flavour marriage, so the tasty purée beautifully complements the chicken.

❶ Pre-heat the oven to gas mark 7, 220°C (425°F). Heat a little oil in a heavy-based frying pan. Season the chicken breasts, place in the pan, skin-side down, and sear on all sides. Remove the chicken and reserve the oil and pan.

❷ Coat the skin-sides of the chicken breasts with the mustard, then dip the coated sides in half of the herbs.

❸ Place the pastry sheet on a lightly floured work surface and cut in half. Roll a lattice cutter over half of each piece, widthways. Place a chicken breast, herb-side down, on top of the lattice and fold over the remaining pastry to enclose it. Trim the edges to seal, then place the parcel on a baking sheet, lattice side up. Repeat with the other breast. Brush with beaten egg and bake for 12–14 minutes until golden.

❹ Cook the swede and carrots in boiling salted water for 10–12 minutes or until tender. Reheat the oil in the reserved pan and cook the onion for 10 minutes or until lightly caramelized.

❺ Make the sauce: place the wine and stock in a pan and bring to the boil. Bubble the liquid down to 1 or 2 tablespoons. Whisk in the butter, remove the pan from the heat and stir in 1 tablespoon of the herbs. Season.

❻ Drain the carrots and swede and whizz in a food processor with the caramelized onion and remaining herbs. Spoon the vegetable purée on to serving plates, add the chicken and drizzle round some sauce to serve.

creamy tarragon turkey

by patrick anthony

4 x 75 g (3 oz) turkey escalopes
1 dessertspoon sunflower oil
50 g (2 oz) unsalted butter
1 large shallot, finely chopped
50 ml (2 fl oz) dry white wine
150 ml (5 fl oz) chicken stock
2 teaspoons fresh lemon juice
½ teaspoon Dijon mustard
1 dessertspoon chopped fresh tarragon
4 tablespoons double cream
2 tomatoes, peeled, seeded and diced
Salt and freshly ground black pepper
Chopped fresh flatleaf parsley, to garnish

This literally takes minutes to prepare and is ideal for a sophisticated eating-out-at-home experience. It would work just as well with two chicken breast fillets halved horizontally.

❶ Heat a large frying pan. Season the turkey escalopes all over. Add the oil and 15 g (½ oz) of butter to the pan and, once the butter starts sizzling, fry the escalopes for 1½ minutes on each side until sealed. Transfer to a plate and keep warm.

❷ Spoon off any excess oil from the pan and add the shallot, stirring to coat. Pour in the wine and reduce to 1 tablespoon of liquid. Mix together the stock, lemon juice and mustard in a jug and pour into the pan, stirring to combine. Bring to the boil and boil fast until the liquid is reduced by half.

❸ Add the tarragon to the pan and whisk in the remaining butter, then add the cream and tomatoes. Just warm the mixture through. Return the turkey to the pan and simmer for 1–2 minutes or until it is tender. Arrange the escalopes on serving plates, spoon over the sauce and sprinkle with parsley to garnish before serving.

warm pasta shells with chicken, basil and pine nuts by phil vickery

175 g (6 oz) dried pasta shells
1 tablespoon olive oil
1 onion, finely chopped
2 small skinless, boneless chicken breast
fillets, cut into 1 cm (½ in) cubes
1 garlic clove, crushed
1 beef tomato, skinned,
seeded and finely chopped
1 tablespoon chopped fresh basil
300 ml (10 fl oz) double cream
25 g (1 oz) pine nuts, toasted
Salt and freshly ground black pepper
2 tablespoons freshly grated Parmesan,
to serve

If you'd like to use fresh pasta for quicker cooking, penne (quills) would be a good alternative. Freshly grated Parmesan is now readily available and bears no resemblance to the nasty dried stuff from a drum.

❶ Bring a large pan of salted water to the boil. Add the pasta shells and cook for 8–10 minutes or until *al dente*.

❷ Heat the oil in a frying pan and fry the onion until softened. Add the chicken and cook for 3 minutes or until the meat has turned opaque. Add the garlic, tomato and basil and cook for 1–2 minutes or until just heated through. Add the cream and bring up to a bubble. Stir in the pine nuts and season generously.

❸ Drain the pasta and return it to the pan. Add the sauce and toss until well combined. Divide the pasta between two warmed wide-rimmed serving bowls and sprinkle with Parmesan before serving.

braised guinea fowl with chestnuts

by richard cawley

25 g (1 oz) unsalted butter
1 small onion, chopped
4 rashers rindless streaky bacon,
roughly chopped
2 skinless guinea fowl breasts,
cut into 2 cm (¾ in) pieces
¼ teaspoon dried sage
200 ml (7 fl oz) Chardonnay or other dry
white wine
10 canned or vacuum-packed
whole peeled chestnuts
2 tablespoons double cream
1 tablespoon snipped fresh chives
Salt and freshly ground black pepper

Major supermarkets now sell guinea fowl all year round. It is my favourite bird and tastes like a very flavoursome chicken.

❶ Heat a heavy-based pan. Add the butter and fry the onion and bacon, stirring occasionally, for 5 minutes or until the onion is lightly coloured and the bacon is beginning to crisp. Add the guinea fowl pieces and sprinkle over the sage, then stir-fry for 3–4 minutes or until the meat is seared all over.

❷ Pour the wine into the pan and add the chestnuts. Season and bring to the boil, then reduce the heat and simmer for 10 minutes or until the guinea fowl is tender and the liquid has reduced by half.

❸ Stir in the cream and chives, season to taste and bring back to just boiling point. Divide between two serving plates.

chicken fajitas with pineapple and chilli salsa by nick nairn

2 skinless, boneless chicken breast fillets

1 dessertspoon garam masala

¼ teaspoon paprika

¼ teaspoon cumin

1 teaspoon chilli powder

1 garlic clove, finely chopped

Juice of 2 limes

3 tablespoons olive oil,

plus extra for char-grilling

1 baby pineapple, peeled, cored and cut into

1 cm (½ in) cubes

1 red finger chilli, seeded and

finely chopped

1 tablespoon chopped fresh coriander

4 soft flour tortillas

2 little gem lettuces, shredded

4 tablespoons crème fraîche

Salt and freshly ground black pepper

hot tip

● To prepare a pineapple, cut off the leaf crown and bottom so that it sits flat. Using a sharp knife, remove the skin by cutting down the length of the fruit, then cut the flesh into wedges lengthways, remove the core and cut into cubes.

I always keep flour tortillas in my store-cupboard – they often come in handy. To make them soft enough for rolling, pop them on a hot griddle or frying pan, or alternatively microwave on high between dampened sheets of kitchen paper for about 30 seconds.

❶ Using a meat mallet, flatten out the chicken breasts, or place the breasts between two sheets of plastic film and bash with a rolling pin.

❷ In a shallow dish, combine the garam masala, paprika, cumin, chilli powder, garlic, salt and pepper, a dessertspoon of lime juice and 1 tablespoon of oil to form a paste. Brush the paste over the chicken breasts and set them aside, covered, for at least 5 minutes and up to 2 hours.

❸ Make the salsa: place the pineapple in a bowl with the chilli, coriander, remaining lime juice and remaining 2 tablespoons of oil. Season generously and mix well.

❹ Heat a griddle pan until very hot and brush with a little oil. Char-grill the chicken breasts for 2–3 minutes or until cooked through. Remove from the pan and thinly slice.

❺ In the pan used to cook the chicken, heat the tortillas by dry-frying them very quickly (about 10 seconds) on each side. Place a little lettuce on each warmed tortilla, top with chicken and a dollop of crème fraîche, then roll up the tortillas and arrange them on serving plates. Serve the salsa on the side.

honey-roast quail on polenta with grape salsa by richard cawley

2 small fresh thyme sprigs

I small garlic clove, halved lengthways

2 lemon or lime wedges

2 oven-ready quail

2 tablespoons clear honey

100 g (4 oz) seedless green grapes, quartered

I small red onion, thinly sliced

I red chilli, seeded and finely chopped

Juice of ½ lemon

I tablespoon chopped fresh flatleaf parsley

350 g (12 oz) packet ready-cooked polenta, cut into 2 cm (¾ in) slices

1–2 tablespoons extra virgin olive oil

Salt and freshly ground black pepper

Quails might seem rather extravagant and somewhat daunting, but they are incredibly easy to cook, not that expensive and readily available. They taste like very delicate chicken – just be careful not to over-cook them as they tend to dry out.

❶ Pre-heat the oven to gas mark 7, 220°C (425°F). Place a thyme sprig, a garlic half and a lemon or lime wedge in the cavity of each quail and brush all over with the honey. Season generously, place in a small roasting tin and roast for about 15 minutes or until cooked through and golden brown. Leave to rest for at least 5 minutes.

❷ Make the salsa: place the grapes, onion, chilli, lemon juice and parsley in a bowl. Season to taste and stir well. Marinate for at least 5 minutes and up to 2 hours to allow the flavours to develop.

❸ Heat a griddle pan. Brush the polenta slices with oil and cook for 3–4 minutes on each side until lightly charred and crisp. Arrange the polenta on plates, place the quails on top and serve with the salsa.

seared chicken with green pea guacamole by james martin

175 g (6 oz) skinless, boneless chicken
breast fillet
3 tablespoons extra virgin olive oil
450 g (1 lb) frozen peas,
thawed and well drained
1 small red onion, finely chopped
10 fresh mint leaves
100 g (4 oz) Greek yoghurt
1 small mild red chilli, seeded and
finely chopped
1 garlic clove, crushed
½ teaspoon ground cumin
Salt and freshly ground black pepper
Handful of fresh coriander leaves,
to garnish

Frozen peas are one of the best frozen foods available as they are packaged when they are still so fresh. This purée also makes a fantastic dip for tortilla chips.

❶ Heat a griddle pan. Slice the chicken breast in half horizontally and place between two pieces of plastic film. Flatten out slightly using a rolling pin, then season generously and brush all over with a little olive oil. Add to the pan and cook for 2–3 minutes on each side or until just tender and cooked through.

❷ Make the guacamole: place the peas in a food processor with the onion and mint and whizz briefly. Add the yoghurt and whizz again until just combined. Tip into a bowl and stir in the chilli, garlic and cumin. Season to taste. This can be served at room temperature or gently heated in a pan for a few minutes.

❸ Divide the guacamole between two serving plates and drizzle over the remaining oil. Garnish with coriander leaves and place the chicken on top to serve.

spatchcock poussins with speedy caponata by richard cawley

1 tablespoon sultanas

2 oven-ready poussins

4 tablespoons extra virgin olive oil

1 aubergine, cut into 2.5 cm (1 in) cubes

2 celery sticks, cut into 1 cm (½ in) lengths

1 small onion, roughly chopped

175 g (6 oz) cherry tomatoes

3 tablespoons red-wine vinegar

1 heaped tablespoon sugar

2 heaped tablespoons tomato purée

50 g (2 oz) large pitted green olives, chopped

2 teaspoons capers, rinsed and drained

50 g (2 oz) can anchovies in olive oil, drained and chopped

25 g (1 oz) pine nuts

1 heaped tablespoon flatleaf parsley leaves, torn if large

Salt and freshly ground black pepper

Poussins are very tender baby chickens, while caponata is a delicious version of ratatouille from Sicily and one of my favourite things to eat. This recipe makes enough caponata to eat cold the next day.

1 Place the sultanas in a bowl and cover with hot water. Soak for at least 5 minutes and up to 1 hour. Pre-heat the grill.

2 Hold each poussin in your hand, breast down. Using kitchen scissors, cut along either side of the backbone, remove the bone and discard. Turn the bird breast-side up. Flatten out by pressing down with the palm of your hand against the breastbone to break it. Brush all over with olive oil, season generously and grill, turning once, for about 15 minutes, or until cooked through and golden brown.

3 Make the caponata: heat the remaining oil in a wok or large frying pan. Add the aubergine, celery and onion and stir-fry for 5 minutes over a high heat or until the vegetables begin to colour. Add the tomatoes, vinegar, sugar, tomato purée, olives, capers and anchovies and stir to combine.

4 Drain the sultanas and stir them into the pan. Season, then reduce the heat, cover and cook, stirring occasionally, for 10–15 minutes until the vegetables are tender.

5 Heat a small frying pan. Add the pine nuts and dry-fry for a few minutes until toasted, stirring occasionally. Remove the lid from the caponata pan, give the mixture a good stir and season, then stir in the pine nuts and parsley. Divide between two serving plates and arrange the poussins on top to serve.

paprika seared chicken on a broccoli stir-fry by kevin woodford

1 large potato, cut into cubes

4 tablespoons olive oil

1 lemon, thinly sliced

8 fresh sage leaves

2 boneless chicken breast fillets, skin on

½ teaspoon ground paprika

150 ml (5 fl oz) chicken stock, made from a cube

1 tablespoon redcurrant jelly

1 teaspoon white-wine vinegar

1 head broccoli, broken into small florets

1 large garlic clove, thinly sliced

4 rashers smoked streaky bacon, finely chopped

Salt and freshly ground black pepper

hot tips

● Fresh stock in tubs is readily available in the chill cabinets of supermarkets and can be used instead of a stock cube.

● Paprika is a very gentle spice which gives colour and depth of flavour to the chicken. Don't confuse it with cayenne pepper which is very hot and gives dishes a real bite!

Cooking this in 20 minutes was really pushing it, but you'll have a lot more time than I did to guarantee fantastic results.

❶ Place the potato in a small pan of boiling salted water. Cover and cook for 10–12 minutes until tender, then drain.

❷ Heat a heavy-based frying pan. Add half the olive oil and quickly sear the lemon slices and sage leaves for 1–2 minutes. Tip out on to a plate and set aside. Dust the chicken skin with paprika, season with salt and sear in the hot pan, skin-side down, for 10–12 minutes or until cooked, turning once.

❸ Place the stock in a small pan and boil rapidly until reduced by half. Add the redcurrant jelly and vinegar and heat gently to melt the jelly, then simmer over a low heat to make a sauce.

❹ Plunge the broccoli into a pan of boiling salted water and blanch for 2 minutes, then drain and refresh under cold running water.

❺ Heat a wok or large frying pan until hot, add the remaining oil, then add the garlic and bacon and stir-fry for 1 minute. Toss in the cooked potatoes and cook until lightly golden. Add the broccoli and stir-fry for 2 minutes. Season to taste.

❻ Return the sage and lemon to a pan. Add the chicken and a splash of sauce. Cook for 1–2 minutes, or until the liquid has evaporated and the chicken is warmed through.

❼ Pile the broccoli, bacon and potato mixture into the centres of two serving plates. Top with the chicken, lemon slices and sage leaves and drizzle round some of the sauce to serve.

bulgar and chicken pilaff with apricots by lesley waters

225 g (8 oz) bulgar wheat

2 tablespoons vegetable oil

I onion, chopped

4 skinless, boneless chicken thighs, well trimmed and cut into I cm (½ in) cubes

I garlic clove, crushed

I heaped teaspoon ground turmeric

I heaped teaspoon ground cumin

I teaspoon ground coriander

100 g (4 oz) ready-to-eat apricots, chopped

2 large carrots, grated

100 g (4 oz) raisins

600 ml (I pint) chicken stock, made from a cube

Salt and freshly ground black pepper

Small bunch of fresh coriander, roughly chopped, to garnish

I lemon, cut into wedges, to serve

This is a superb, exotic-flavoured dish that adds real interest to supermarket chicken pieces.

❶ Place the bulgar wheat in a bowl and pour over enough boiling water to cover. Set aside for 5 minutes or according to packet instructions.

❷ Meanwhile, heat the oil in a large frying pan, then add the onion, stirring to coat. Cover and cook for 2–3 minutes until softened.

❸ Add the chicken, garlic and spices to the pan, then cover and cook for 4–5 minutes. Stir in the apricots, carrots and raisins. Pour in the stock and bring up to a gentle simmer until the chicken is cooked through and tender.

❹ Just before serving, drain the bulgar wheat of any excess water, add to the pan and heat through until almost all the liquid has evaporated. Season to taste. Spoon some of the pilaff on to each serving plate. Sprinkle with coriander and serve with lemon wedges.

hot tip

● Bulgar, a lightly cooked and crushed wheat, is equally delicious eaten hot or cold. If you prefer you could use couscous or cooked rice for this pilaff.

asian pork lettuce rolls

by antony worrall thompson

2 garlic cloves, finely chopped

½ teaspoon salt

1 teaspoon ground black pepper

4 tablespoons chopped fresh coriander

1 tablespoon fresh lime juice

Groundnut or sunflower oil, for frying

225 g (8 oz) pork tenderloin fillet,
cut into thin strips with the grain

2 tablespoons chopped natural peanuts,
skins removed

2 tablespoons canned bamboo shoots,
drained and chopped

2 tablespoons Thai fish sauce (nam pla) or
dark soy sauce

1 tablespoon clear honey

1 bird's eye chilli, finely chopped

3 shallots, thinly sliced

2 large oranges, segmented

2 tablespoons chopped fresh mint

2 little gem lettuces, separated into leaves

Crispy noodles, to serve

This is one of my favourite dishes at my local Chinese restaurant. It's great finger food and the crisp lettuce wrapping sets off the spicy pork beautifully.

❶ Heat a large frying pan. Mix together the garlic, salt, pepper, 2 tablespoons of coriander and the lime juice in a small bowl. Add 2 tablespoons of oil to the pan, tip in the garlic mixture and stir-fry for 30 seconds, then add the pork and stir-fry for a few minutes until sealed and lightly browned.

❷ Add the peanuts, bamboo shoots, Thai or soy sauce, honey and chilli to the pork mixture and cook for 4–5 minutes until the liquid has nearly evaporated.

❸ Heat at least 5 cm (2 in) of oil in a pan or a deep-fat fryer to 190°C (375°F). Add two of the shallots and deep-fry for 30 seconds or until crispy. Drain well on kitchen paper.

❹ Place the remaining shallot in a bowl with the orange segments and a heaped teaspoon each of mint and coriander. Mix well and pile into the middle of a large plate or platter. Stir the remaining mint and coriander into the pork and fill the lettuce leaves with the mixture. Arrange the leaves around the orange salad. Garnish with the deep-fried shallots and crispy noodles.

inverted cheeseburger with hot ketchup by antony worrall thompson

25 g (1 oz) Roquefort cheese
25 g (1 oz) unsalted butter, softened
1 tablespoon snipped fresh chives
1 red onion
3 tablespoons olive oil
1 leek, finely chopped
2 garlic cloves, crushed
1 red chilli, seeded and finely chopped
200 g (7 oz) can chopped tomatoes
350 g (12 oz) minced beef
2 teaspoons coarsely ground black pepper
1 tablespoon sunflower oil
1 tablespoon chopped fresh basil
2 burger buns, split in half
1 pickled cucumber, sliced
2 tomatoes, sliced
1 little gem lettuce, separated into leaves
Salt and freshly ground black pepper

hot tips

● Store any remaining ketchup in an air-tight container in the fridge for 4–5 days.
● Ideally the mince used for burgers should contain at least 20 per cent fat. This adds to the flavour and stops them from drying out when cooking.

These fantastic burgers with all the trimmings make a perfect speedy supper. They would also work very well on the barbecue.

❶ In a small bowl, mash together the cheese and butter, season, then mix in the chives. Place in the fridge until needed.

❷ Halve the onion, cut one half into thin slices and reserve for garnishing, then finely chop the other half. Place the olive oil in a pan and fry the chopped onion and leek for a few minutes until softened. Add the garlic and chilli, season generously and cook for another minute. Pour in the tomatoes and bubble gently for 8–10 minutes or until the ketchup is reduced and slightly thickened.

❸ Divide the beef into two and, using your hands, shape into patties. Make a deep indentation in both burgers and place a 25 g (1 oz) nugget of the butter and cheese mixture in each hole, pushing the beef back around the mixture so that it is well sealed. Sprinkle 1 teaspoon of pepper and a good pinch of salt all over each burger. Chill until ready to cook.

❹ Heat a frying pan until hot. Add the sunflower oil and cook the burgers for 4 minutes on each side for rare, 6 minutes each side for medium and 8–9 minutes for well done. Stir the basil into the tomato ketchup.

❺ Place the two burger bun bottoms on serving plates with the burgers on top. Surround with the bun tops, pickled cucumber, tomato and onion slices and lettuce leaves and serve with the warm ketchup.

pork satay

by antony worrall thompson

2 large garlic cloves, chopped

I red chilli, seeded and chopped

I cm (½ in) piece fresh root ginger,
peeled and chopped

¼ teaspoon Chinese five spice powder or

¼ teaspoon shrimp paste

50 g (2 oz) natural peanuts,
skins removed

Good pinch of salt

2 tablespoons sunflower oil

400 g (14 oz) can coconut milk

450 g (1 lb) pork leg, trimmed and cut Into
2 cm (¾ in) chunks

FOR THE SAUCE

2 tablespoons sunflower oil

100 g (4 oz) natural peanuts,
skins removed

2 shallots, finely chopped

I garlic clove, finely chopped

I teaspoon Chinese five spice powder or I
teaspoon shrimp paste

Pinch of chilli powder

Good pinch of salt

I tablespoon fresh lemon juice

I teaspoon light muscovado sugar

Shrimp paste gives this dish a particularly authentic flavour. It is readily available in most oriental stores, in small tubs, and once opened keeps for quite a while stored in the fridge.

❶ Place the garlic, chilli, ginger, five spice powder or shrimp paste, peanuts and salt in a food processor and whizz until smooth. Heat a pan, add the oil, then add the garlic mixture. Cook for 1 minute or until the mixture turns golden and smells fragrant. Pour in the coconut milk and simmer for 5 minutes until thickened, then tip into a non-metallic dish and cool. Add the pork and marinate for at least 5 minutes or up to 24 hours covered in the fridge.

❷ Make the sauce: heat a pan, add half the oil and fry the peanuts for 1–2 minutes until sizzling and lightly golden. Place in a food processor and blend to a powder, then tip into a bowl. Place the shallots, garlic, five spice powder or shrimp paste, chilli powder and salt in a pestle and mortar or food processor and blend to a paste.

❸ Add the remaining oil to a pan and tip in the shallot paste. Cook for 30 seconds, stirring, then pour in 300 ml (10 fl oz) of water. Bring to the boil, then stir in the peanut powder, lemon juice and sugar. Season and simmer for 4–5 minutes until thickened, then leave to cool.

❹ Pre-heat a griddle pan. Arrange the pork on six 15 cm (6 in) bamboo skewers which have been soaked in water for 30 minutes. Char-grill for 8–10 minutes or until cooked through. Divide the pork between two serving plates, then pour the sauce into dipping bowls and serve.

thai pork burgers

by ross burden

400 g (14 oz) pork mince

2 teaspoons sesame oil

2 teaspoons dark soy sauce

2 teaspoons Thai fish sauce (nam pla) or
Worcestershire sauce

2 tablespoons chopped fresh coriander

1 green chilli, seeded and finely chopped

Grated rind of 2 limes or 6 kaffir lime
leaves, finely shredded

4 tablespoons fresh white breadcrumbs

Freshly ground black pepper

75 g (3 oz) sesame seeds

Burger buns, salad and condiments,
to serve

These burgers can be made a few hours ahead of time, covered with plastic film and placed in the fridge until ready to cook. I like to serve them with a dollop of mayonnaise that has lots of chopped coriander stirred in, crisp lettuce leaves and slices of juicy tomatoes.

❶ Place the mince in a bowl with all the ingredients down to and including the breadcrumbs. Season with black pepper, mix well and form into two balls. Pre-heat a griddle pan to smoking hot.

❷ Place the sesame seeds on a flat plate and roll the balls in them until well coated. Flatten the balls into burger shapes and char-grill them, turning occasionally, for 8–10 minutes until cooked through. Serve in a burger bun with salad and your favourite accompaniments.

hot tip

● Kaffir lime leaves are part of the lemon grass family. All of these plants taste of lemon or lime due to the presence of citric oils. Kaffir lime can also be used to flavour fish dishes.

oriental beef salad

by antony worrall thompson

225 g (8 oz) piece Scottish rump or
sirloin steak
1 tablespoon sunflower oil
2 tablespoons fresh lime juice
2 tablespoons dark soy sauce or Thai
fish sauce (nam pla)
2 tablespoons clear honey
1 small leek, thinly sliced
½ red chilli, seeded and finely chopped
1 garlic clove, finely chopped
3 tomatoes, cut into wedges and seeded
1 little gem lettuce
4 spring onions, thinly sliced
1 small cucumber, peeled, halved
lengthways, seeded and
cut into 2.5 cm (1 in) chunks
1 tablespoon shredded fresh mint
Good handful of flatleaf parsley and fresh
coriander leaves
Salt and freshly ground black pepper
Fresh chives and mint sprigs, to garnish

Slightly sweet and sour, this packs a real flavour punch – enough to make a robust partner for some plain boiled rice or noodles.

❶ Heat a frying pan until smoking hot. Season the beef. Add the oil to the pan and fry the beef for 4–5 minutes on each side. Transfer to a warmed plate and rest for at least 5 minutes, then slice thinly across the grain.

❷ Meanwhile, place the lime juice, soy or Thai sauce and honey in a pan. Mix well and simmer for 2 minutes or until heated through. Stir in the leek, chilli, garlic and tomato wedges and simmer gently to just warm through.

❸ Cut the lettuce in half, shred half and reserve the remaining leaves for garnish. In a large bowl, combine the spring onions, cucumber and shredded lettuce. Fold in the warm ingredients, then the beef, mint and parsley and coriander leaves. Toss together and season to taste. Arrange the whole lettuce leaves around the edges of two serving plates and pile the beef mixture in the centres. Garnish with chives and mint sprigs, to serve.

hot tip

● Opt for steaks with a marbling – little rivulets – of fat. These tenderize the meat and give it more flavour.

71

carbonara

by ross burden

1 tablespoon olive oil
150 g (5 oz) pancetta
1 onion, finely chopped
1 garlic clove, crushed
350 g (12 oz) fresh tagliatelle
1 egg yolk
150 ml (5 fl oz) double cream
1 tablespoon chopped fresh
flatleaf parsley
Salt and freshly ground black pepper
1 heaped tablespoon freshly grated
Parmesan, to serve

hot tip

● Parmesan is a very hard Italian 'grana' cheese made from unpasteurized semi-skimmed cows' milk. The younger it is, the softer it is. At three to four years old it is darker, drier and very hard – almost crystallized in the centre. It is best bought in a wedge and freshly grated.

I'm a real pasta fan and this variation on a classic recipe is packed with flavour and texture. Be warned, though – my portions are pretty generous and it's a very filling dish.

❶ Heat the oil in a pan. Fry the pancetta until the fat starts to run. Add the onion and cook for 3–4 minutes or until the onion is soft and the pancetta has started to brown. Add the garlic and cook for 2 minutes.

❷ Bring a large pan of salted water to the boil. Place the tagliatelle in the water and cook for 2 minutes or until *al dente*. Drain the pasta and return it to the pan.

❸ Whisk the egg yolk into the cream and add to the pancetta and onion mixture, then reduce the sauce slightly before pouring it over the tagliatelle. Add the parsley and toss until combined. Season to taste. Spoon into two warmed wide-rimmed serving bowls and sprinkle with Parmesan to serve.

cheesy empanadas with mojo sauce by paul rankin

2 sun-dried red peppers
100 g (4 oz) plain flour, plus extra
for dusting
40 g (1½ oz) chilled unsalted butter, diced
3–4 tablespoons warm water
50 g (2 oz) potato, finely diced
2 spring onions, finely chopped
50 g (2 oz) Cheddar, grated
50 g (2 oz) chorizo sausage, diced
Groundnut oil, for deep-frying
1 egg yolk, lightly beaten, to glaze
1 garlic clove, roughly chopped
¼ teaspoon ground cumin
¼ teaspoon ground coriander
½ teaspoon hot paprika
1–2 tablespoons red-wine vinegar
6 tablespoons extra virgin olive oil
Salt and freshly ground black pepper
Fresh herb sprigs, to garnish

For a vegetarian alternative, omit the chorizo and increase the quantity of potato, adding a finely chopped red chilli for extra bite.

❶ Roughly tear up the peppers into a bowl and pour over boiling water to reconstitute them. Place the flour in a food processor with a pinch of salt and 25 g (1 oz) of butter. Whizz for 10 seconds, then slowly pour 2–3 tablespoons of warm water through the feeder tube until the mixture starts to come together. Turn out on to a lightly floured board and knead briefly. Divide into six even-sized balls, cover with a clean tea towel and leave to rest.

❷ Meanwhile, melt the remaining butter in a pan. Add the diced potato and cook, stirring occasionally, for 6–8 minutes until just tender. Add the spring onions and cook for a further minute, then remove from the heat and stir in the Cheddar and chorizo. Season and leave to cool.

❸ Heat the oil in a large pan or a deep-fat fryer to 190°C (375°F). Place the dough balls on a lightly floured surface and roll out into 12 cm (5 in) circles. Brush the circles all over with the egg yolk, divide the potato mixture among them, then fold each one over to form a half moon shape. Crimp the edges together and deep-fry in batches for 3–4 minutes. Drain well on kitchen paper.

❹ Drain and roughly chop the peppers and place them in a food processor with the garlic, cumin, coriander, paprika, vinegar and seasoning. Whizz until well combined then, with the motor running, pour in the olive oil to make a smooth sauce, adding a little water if the sauce is too thick. Flood the serving plates with the sauce, arrange the empanadas on top and garnish with herb sprigs.

mini moussakas

by brian turner

1 large potato, sliced

1 tablespoon sunflower oil

1 onion, finely chopped

1 garlic clove, crushed

225 g (8 oz) lean minced lamb

1 teaspoon ground cumin

1 dessertspoon tomato purée

50 ml (2 fl oz) dry white wine

50 ml (2 fl oz) chicken or lamb stock

1 courgette, sliced

1 tablespoon olive oil

25 g (1 oz) unsalted butter

25 g (1 oz) plain flour

300 ml (10 fl oz) milk

½ teaspoon freshly grated nutmeg

1 tablespoon chopped fresh
flatleaf parsley

4 plum tomatoes, peeled,
seeded and finely diced

50 g (2 oz) Cheddar, grated

Salt and freshly ground black pepper

Fresh flatleaf parsley, to garnish

Minced lamb is now readily available in all supermarkets. It's very good value for money and often has more flavour than minced beef.

❶ Bring a pan of salted water to the boil. Add the potato slices and par-boil for 6–8 minutes or until they are tender, then drain well and set aside.

❷ Heat the sunflower oil in a heavy-based pan. Fry the onion for 2–3 minutes until softened, then add the garlic and cook for 1–2 minutes until softened.

❸ Add the lamb to the onion and cook for 2–3 minutes until the lamb is lightly browned, then add the cumin, tomato purée, white wine and stock. Season generously and mix to combine. Bring to a simmer, then reduce the heat and bubble gently for 3–4 minutes or until the mixture is quite thick and dry.

❹ Heat a griddle pan. Toss the courgette slices in the olive oil, season and char-grill for 2–3 minutes or until tender.

❺ Melt the butter in a heavy-based pan, remove from the heat and add the flour, stirring continuously. Return to the heat and cook for 1 minute, stirring, then gradually pour in the milk, stirring until smooth. Add the nutmeg, season and simmer for 2–3 minutes until the sauce has thickened.

❻ Pre-heat the grill to hot. Stir the parsley into the lamb and season. Divide the lamb between two individual ovenproof dishes or two 10 cm (4 in) metal cooking rings, add a layer of courgettes, then the potatoes. Top with the tomatoes, pour over the sauce and scatter over the cheese. Grill for 3–4 minutes or until golden and bubbling. Garnish with parsley.

pork cannelloni

by phil vickery

1 tablespoon olive oil
1 onion, finely chopped
300 g (10 oz) lean minced pork
40 g (1½ oz) plain flour
½ teaspoon dried oregano
½ teaspoon ground cumin
200 g (7 oz) can chopped tomatoes
1 tablespoon chopped fresh coriander
6 fresh lasagne sheets
40 g (1½ oz) unsalted butter
450 ml (15 fl oz) milk
*1 tablespoon chopped fresh
flatleaf parsley*
1 tablespoon wholegrain mustard
2 tablespoons freshly grated Parmesan
Salt and freshly ground black pepper
Fresh green salad, to serve

hot tips

● It's a little known fact that lean pork has less fat per 100 g (4 oz) than cottage cheese – and it is very good for you.
● You can completely assemble this dish, cool it and then freeze it, ready to cook from frozen when needed.

Fresh pasta is readily available in supermarket chill cabinets in an ever-growing range of shapes and sizes. When draining fresh lasagne sheets, remember that they will not get sticky if placed in a warm colander.

❶ Pre-heat the oven to gas mark 7, 220°C (425°F). Heat the oil in a pan, add the onion and cook for a few minutes until softened. Add the pork and fry for 3 minutes or until the meat has turned opaque. Add 1 teaspoon of the flour, the oregano, cumin, tomatoes and coriander to the pan and cook for 4–5 minutes or until nicely thickened.

❷ Bring a large pan of salted water to the boil. Blanch the lasagne for about 2 minutes, or until *al dente*, then drain well and refresh under cold running water.

❸ Melt the butter in a small pan, add the remaining flour and cook for a few seconds until heated through. Slowly pour in the milk, stirring continuously. Add the parsley and mustard, season, then reduce the heat and simmer for 2 minutes until the sauce has thickened.

❹ Divide the pork mixture between the lasagne sheets. Roll up and place in an ovenproof dish. Pour over the sauce, sprinkle with the Parmesan and bake for 10 minutes or until bubbling and golden. Divide between two warmed serving plates and serve at once with fresh green salad.

sausage goulash

by antony worrall thompson

175 g (6 oz) long-grain rice, well rinsed

2 tablespoons sunflower oil

225 g (8 oz) pork sausages, cut into
2.5 cm (1 in) pieces

100 g (4 oz) chorizo sausage, cut into
2.5 cm (1 in) pieces

15 g (½ oz) unsalted butter

1 onion, roughly chopped

2 garlic cloves, crushed

1 small red pepper, seeded and
roughly chopped

1 tablespoon hot paprika

1 bay leaf

¼ teaspoon dried oregano

400 g (14 oz) can chopped tomatoes in
rich tomato sauce

150 ml (5 fl oz) chicken or beef stock

4 heaped tablespoons Greek yoghurt or
soured cream

Salt and freshly ground black pepper

1 teaspoon snipped fresh chives,
to garnish

Try to buy good-quality sausages for this recipe – you'll find it makes all the difference. I like to serve this with rice but some buttered noodles or tagliatelle would also work very well.

❶ Place the rice in a pan with 350 ml (12 fl oz) of water, add a pinch of salt, cover and simmer for 10–12 minutes or according to packet instructions.

❷ Heat a frying pan, add half the oil and fry the pork sausages for 3–4 minutes until lightly browned, then add the chorizo and cook for 1–2 minutes until sizzling. Remove the sausages from the pan and drain on kitchen paper.

❸ Meanwhile, heat another pan and add the remaining oil and the butter. Add the onion, garlic and red pepper and cook for 3 minutes until the onion has softened. Add the paprika and fry for 1 minute, stirring, then add the bay leaf, oregano, tomatoes, stock and seasoning and bring to the boil.

❹ Add the sausages to the onion and tomato mixture and simmer, uncovered, for 10 minutes or until the sauce has thickened and reduced. Stir in the yoghurt or soured cream and season to taste. Divide the rice between two serving plates, spoon over the sausage goulash and sprinkle with chives to serve.

aromatic beef stir-fry

by antony worrall thompson

*225 g (8 oz) piece sirloin steak,
well trimmed*
3 tablespoons dark soy sauce
1½ tablespoons cornflour
2 tablespoons dark muscovado sugar
1 teaspoon grated fresh root ginger
2 garlic cloves, finely chopped
½ teaspoon dried chilli flakes
8 spring onions, cut into 1 cm (½ in) slices
2 tablespoons dry sherry or rice wine
*1 tablespoon rice vinegar or
white-wine vinegar*
150 ml (5 fl oz) chicken stock
*175 g (6 oz) mixed green vegetables (such
as asparagus, sugar snap peas, broccoli,
Chinese cabbage), all cut into
2.5 cm (1 in) pieces*
2 tablespoons vegetable oil
1 tablespoon torn fresh coriander
2 tablespoons torn fresh basil
Salt and freshly ground black pepper
Plain boiled rice or noodles, to serve

**Simple, but very stylish, this dish would be
excellent as a main course for a special dinner.
All the components can be prepared a few
hours in advance.**

❶ Bring a large pan of salted water to the boil. Cut the steak
into 5 cm (2 in) strips, then into 5 mm (¼ in) slices. Combine
half the soy sauce, cornflour and sugar in a bowl. Fold in the beef
slices and mix well to coat. Marinate for at least 5 minutes and
up to 12 hours covered in the fridge.

❷ Mix together the ginger, garlic, chilli flakes and spring onions
in a bowl and set aside. Place the remaining soy sauce and sugar
in a jug with the sherry or rice wine, vinegar and stock. Mix well
to combine and set aside.

❸ Blanch all the vegetables in the boiling water (asparagus for
3 minutes, Chinese leaves and broccoli 2 minutes, sugar snap
peas 1 minute).

❹ Heat a wok until smoking. Add half the oil and fry the beef for
2–4 minutes until well sealed and lightly browned. Tip it out on
to a warmed plate and keep warm. Add the remaining oil and
increase the heat. Add the ginger and garlic mixture and stir-fry
for 1 minute, then pour in the stock mixture and bring to a simmer.

❺ Combine the remaining cornflour in a small bowl with a little
water to form a paste, then stir into the wok. Cook for 30
seconds or until the sauce becomes glossy and thickens. Check the
seasoning. Return the beef to the wok with the blanched vegetables,
coriander and basil and heat through. Serve immediately with rice
or noodles.

raj fruit-filled pork chops

by brian turner

50 g (2 oz) unsalted butter

I small Granny Smith apple, peeled, cored and diced

¼ teaspoon medium curry powder

Good pinch of ground cumin

I small banana, diced

I heaped teaspoon sultanas

I teaspoon chopped fresh flatleaf parsley

2 x 150 g (5 oz) pork loin chops, trimmed of excess fat

I tablespoon sunflower oil

450 g (1 lb) potatoes, cubed

3–4 tablespoons Greek yoghurt

Salt and freshly ground black pepper

Fresh parsley sprigs, to garnish

These can be made well in advance and kept covered in the fridge until needed. I like them best with mashed potatoes but they would also be great with some lightly spiced rice.

❶ Pre-heat the oven to gas mark 6, 200°C (400°F). Heat a frying pan and add 15 g (½ oz) of butter. Add the apple and cook for 2–3 minutes, then sprinkle with the curry powder and cumin and cook for 30 seconds. Add the banana, sultanas and parsley and heat through, then toss to combine without breaking up any of the fruit.

❷ Carefully make a deep pocket in the meat side of each pork chop, being careful not to pierce through the flesh. Divide the fruit mixture between the pockets and secure each one with a cocktail stick.

❸ Heat a knob of butter and the oil in an ovenproof frying pan. Add the stuffed pork chops to the pan and cook over a fairly high heat for 1–2 minutes on each side until sealed and lightly browned. Transfer the pan to the oven and cook the chops for 8–10 minutes or until they are tender and cooked through, then rest for 5 minutes. Remove the cocktail sticks.

❹ Meanwhile, cook the potatoes in a pan of boiling salted water for 10 minutes or until tender. Drain them and mash with a potato masher, then beat in the remaining butter and the yoghurt. Season to taste and divide between two serving plates. Arrange the pork chops on top and garnish with parsley sprigs.

aromatic lamb and spinach balti

by richard cawley

2 tablespoons vegetable oil

I onion, sliced

Good pinch of salt

½ teaspoon cumin seeds

2 garlic cloves, crushed

I teaspoon minced ginger from a jar

2 teaspoons medium curry powder

1–2 teaspoons garam masala

300 g (10 oz) lamb neck fillet, cut into bite-size pieces

400 g (14 oz) can chopped tomatoes

75 g (3 oz) fresh baby spinach

2 heaped tablespoons Greek yoghurt

Handful of fresh coriander leaves, to garnish

Chapatis or naan bread and a selection of chutneys, to serve (optional)

hot tips

● You could also use cubed leg or shoulder of lamb for this dish.

● The secret of a good curry base is to cook the herbs and spices before adding the meat. Cooking brings out their true flavour, making them more aromatic than they are in their raw state, and the taste of the finished dish is vastly improved.

Originally slow-cooked dishes from the northernmost part of Pakistan, baltis evolved via Birmingham into rapid stir-fries. They are cooked and served in a two-handled *balti* or *karhai* – and are traditionally eaten with chapatis (see page 80) or naan bread. A balti is the one curry that is not served with rice.

❶ Heat the oil in a wok or heavy-based frying pan. Add the onion with the salt and cook for 5 minutes or until softened and just beginning to brown at the edges.

❷ Stir in the cumin seeds and cook for 20 seconds, then add the garlic and ginger and stir-fry for 30 seconds. Add the curry powder and garam masala and cook for another minute or so, stirring occasionally.

❸ Add the lamb to the pan and stir-fry for a few minutes until well coated and sealed. Pour in the tomatoes and bring to a simmer, then cook for 5 minutes or until the lamb is tender. Stir in the spinach and yoghurt and cook, stirring occasionally, for 5 minutes or until the spinach is wilted and tender. Garnish with coriander and serve with home-made chapatis or naan bread and chutneys, if liked.

chapatis

by richard cawley

150 g (5 oz) wholemeal flour
25 g (1 oz) plain flour
120 ml (4 fl oz) warm water
2 tablespoons sunflower oil
Salt and freshly ground black pepper

hot tip

● Make the chapatis just before serving as they tend to stiffen and become tough if kept for too long.

These take no time at all to prepare and are just as good as any you will have tasted! Use them to mop up your favourite curry or serve them as part of an Indian meal.

❶ Sift the flours, salt and pepper into a food processor, then tip in any flakes of bran which may remain in the sieve. With the motor running, pour in the water and half the oil to form a soft dough.

❷ Turn the dough out on to a floured surface and knead briefly until smooth; cover with a clean tea towel and set aside for about 5 minutes.

❸ Heat a little oil in a large frying pan. Take a golf-ball-size piece of dough and roll it out to a 10 cm (4 in) round. Cook in the pan for 2 minutes on each side until golden and a little puffed. Drain the chapati on kitchen paper and keep warm in a clean tea towel. Repeat with the remaining dough. Serve warm.

lamb koftas with baba ghanoush

by james martin

Olive oil, for frying
1 large aubergine, halved and flesh scored
in a criss-cross pattern
300 g (10 oz) lean minced lamb
2 spring onions, finely chopped
1 egg yolk
3 tablespoons chopped fresh parsley
1 teaspoon ground cumin
1 canned anchovy fillet, drained and finely
chopped (optional)
1 small garlic clove, crushed
Good squeeze of lemon juice
12 fresh mint leaves
1 tablespoon light tahini paste
5 walnut halves
5 tablespoons olive oil
2 tablespoons wholegrain mustard
Grated rind and juice of 1 lime
1 plum tomato, peeled, seeded and diced
Salt and freshly ground black pepper

Tahini is a sesame seed paste which can be bought toasted or untoasted. I prefer to use the toasted variety to make this variation on aubergine caviar.

❶ Heat 1 cm (½ in) of olive oil in a large frying pan. Add the aubergine halves to the pan and cook flesh-side down for 5 minutes, then turn them over and cook for 2 minutes until softened and tender. Remove from the pan and leave to cool a little.

❷ Place the lamb, spring onions, egg yolk, parsley, cumin and anchovy fillet, if using, in a bowl. Season and mix well. Divide the mixture in half and shape into two small, thick patties.

❸ Heat a frying pan. Brush the patties lightly with oil and cook them in the pan for 4 minutes each side for rare, 6 minutes each side for medium, and 8–9 minutes for well done.

❹ Roughly chop the aubergine flesh and place in a food processor with the garlic, lemon juice, half of the mint, and the tahini and walnuts. Season and add 3 tablespoons of oil, then whizz for about 20 seconds to make a rough purée. Divide the purée between two serving plates and place a lamb burger on top.

❺ Roughly chop the remaining mint and add to the pan you have just cooked the lamb in, then add the mustard, lime rind and juice, tomato dice and remaining oil and heat through gently to make a sauce. Season to taste and drizzle over the lamb and around the plate.

fiery cocktail sausages with onion marmalade by brian turner

25 g (1 oz) unsalted butter
2 tablespoons sunflower oil
350 g (12 oz) red onions, thinly sliced
150 ml (5 fl oz) red wine
1 tablespoon red-wine vinegar
50 g (2 oz) light muscovado sugar
225 g (8 oz) lean minced pork
50 g (2 oz) fresh white breadcrumbs
1 small red chilli,
seeded and finely chopped
1 heaped teaspoon grated fresh
root ginger
1 heaped tablespoon snipped fresh chives
About 60 cm (2 ft) sausage skin (optional)
Salt and freshly ground black pepper
Fresh chives, to garnish

This recipe uses a sausage machine, which you can buy from most good kitchen supply shops or by mail order from kitchenware companies. However, it's not a necessity and you can make the sausages by hand.

❶ Heat a frying pan and add half the butter and half the oil. Add the onions and cook over a high heat for a few minutes, stirring constantly, until lightly coloured. Pour in the wine, then add the vinegar, sugar and seasoning, stirring until well combined. Bring to a simmer, then reduce the heat and cook for 10 minutes or until almost all the liquid has evaporated. Season to taste.

❷ Meanwhile, place the pork in a bowl with the breadcrumbs, chilli, ginger and chives and season generously. Mix well, feed into a sausage machine and fill the skin, twisting it into 4 cm (1½ in) lengths. Alternatively, divide the mixture into 12 pieces and shape into 4 cm (1½ in) lengths, using the palms of your hands. If you have used a sausage machine plunge the filled sausage skin into a pan of boiling water and simmer for 4 minutes, then drain well on kitchen paper before snipping it into individual sausages.

❸ Heat a frying pan with the remaining butter and oil and fry the sausages made by machine for 2–3 minutes (if you have made them by hand they'll need 6–8 minutes), until lightly golden and cooked through. Drain on kitchen paper. Divide the onion marmalade between two serving plates and arrange the sausages on top. Garnish with fresh chives, to serve.

quick lamb cobbler

by brian turner

350 g (12 oz) lamb neck fillet, cut into
1 cm (½ in) cubes
2 tablespoons plain flour,
seasoned with salt and pepper
3 tablespoons olive oil
1 onion, finely chopped
1 large carrot, diced
1 small swede, diced
100 g (4 oz) plain flour,
plus extra for dusting
1 teaspoon baking powder
1 tablespoon chopped fresh sage
1 egg
2 tablespoons milk
1 teaspoon paprika
300 ml (10 fl oz) lamb stock
Salt and freshly ground black pepper

For a rich, tasty, succulent winter warmer, look no further than this. The scone topping is the perfect foil to the lamb as it is as light as a feather.

❶ Pre-heat the oven to gas mark 5, 190°C (375°F). Toss the lamb in the seasoned flour until each piece is well coated. Heat 2 tablespoons of oil in a heavy-based pan and fry the lamb for 2–3 minutes until well sealed and lightly browned. Tip on to a warmed plate and keep warm.

❷ Add the remaining oil to the pan and fry the onion for 2–3 minutes until just softened, then add the carrot and swede and fry for 4–5 minutes or until they are beginning to soften.

❸ Meanwhile, sift the flour and baking powder into a bowl and season generously, then stir in the sage. Make a well in the centre and break in the egg, then add the milk and mix well until you have a soft dough – if the mixture is too sticky add a little more flour.

❹ Return the lamb to the pan with the paprika, then pour in the stock. Season to taste and stir well to combine. Bring to the boil, lower the heat and simmer for a few minutes until the liquid has slightly thickened. Transfer to an ovenproof dish.

❺ Tip the dough out on to a lightly floured work surface and gently roll out a 13 cm (5 in) circle. Divide the dough into four triangles and arrange on top of the lamb. Bake for 15–20 minutes or until the scones are well risen and lightly golden.

barbecued lamb with french bean salad and tzatziki by ross burden

7 tablespoons extra virgin olive oil

4 garlic cloves, finely sliced

1 teaspoon roughly chopped fresh rosemary

1 teaspoon roughly chopped fresh thyme

Juice of 1 lemon

2 lamb neck fillets, well trimmed

1 tablespoon baby capers, drained and well rinsed

1 tablespoon balsamic vinegar

1 tablespoon chopped fresh flatleaf parsley

1 small cucumber, peeled, halved, seeded and very thinly sliced

225 g (8 oz) French beans, trimmed

5 cm (2 in) slice of bread (from a large farmhouse loaf), quartered, and crusts removed

120 ml (4 fl oz) red wine

175 ml (6 fl oz) lamb or vegetable stock

1 tablespoon chopped fresh dill

250 g (9 oz) Greek yoghurt

Salt and freshly ground black pepper

This dish captures all that is lovely about 'sunshine' summer ingredients.

❶ Pre-heat the barbecue, if using. In a shallow, non-metallic dish, mix together 4 tablespoons of olive oil, half the garlic and the rosemary, thyme and lemon juice. Season with pepper. Add the lamb and coat well. Cover and marinate for at least 5 minutes.

❷ Place the capers, balsamic vinegar, parsley, 1 garlic clove and the remaining olive oil in a bowl. Season and mix well. Salt the cucumber and leave to drain in a sieve set over a bowl.

❸ Blanch the beans in boiling salted water for 3–4 minutes or until just tender. Drain, refresh under cold running water and toss in the dressing while they are still warm.

❹ Heat a griddle pan, if using, until smoking hot. Drain the lamb fillets well, reserving the marinade, and cook on the barbecue or in the pan for 8–10 minutes, turning them occasionally, until completely tender. Rest under foil for a few minutes. Hollow out the four bread cubes, then place them on the barbecue or in the pan and cook on all sides until crisp and lightly charred.

❺ Place the reserved marinade in a small pan with the red wine and reduce to 1 tablespoon. Add the stock and reduce again until the sauce is thickened and bubbling.

❻ Make the tzatziki: rinse the cucumber and squeeze dry in a clean tea towel. Combine with the remaining garlic, the dill and the yoghurt. Season and mix well.

❼ Place two bread boxes on each serving plate and fill with the beans. Arrange the lamb on the side of each plate and pour over the red wine sauce. Serve the tzatziki on the side.

pork fillet towers provençal

by brian turner

75 g (3 oz) unsalted butter

1 shallot, chopped

300 ml (10 fl oz) red wine

150 ml (5 fl oz) chicken stock

1 garlic clove, crushed

2 large plum tomatoes, peeled, seeded and diced

¼ teaspoon fresh thyme leaves

50 ml (2 fl oz) dry white wine

4 x 50 g (2 oz) pork tenderloin fillet medallions

1 courgette, thickly sliced on the diagonal

2 tablespoons olive oil

Salt and freshly ground black pepper

1 heaped teaspoon chopped fresh flatleaf parsley, to garnish

A sophisticated dish, perfect for entertaining or just as a treat. It really takes no time at all to prepare and the results will never fail to impress.

❶ Pre-heat the oven to gas mark 6, 200°C (400°F). Make the sauce: heat a pan, add 25 g (1 oz) of butter and cook the shallot for 2–3 minutes until softened but not coloured. Pour in the red wine and reduce until all the liquid has evaporated, then pour in the stock and reduce again by half. Season and whisk in 25 g (1 oz) of butter.

❷ Meanwhile, heat a pan, add 25 g (1 oz) of butter, then stir in the garlic and tomatoes and cook for 2–3 minutes. Add the thyme, white wine and seasoning and cook for a few minutes until the sauce has reduced.

❸ Drizzle the pork and courgette slices with oil. Heat a griddle pan, then season the pork and cook the medallions for 2–3 minutes on each side until cooked through. Rest for 5 minutes in a warm place. Season the courgette slices and cook for 2–3 minutes or until lightly charred and tender.

❹ Place two 10 cm (4 in) buttered metal cooking rings on a baking sheet and arrange a third of the courgettes in the bottom in an overlapping layer. Spoon over a third of the tomatoes and top with a pork medallion. Repeat these layers, then finish with a layer of courgettes and a layer of tomatoes. Bake for 5 minutes until heated through, then carefully remove the rings. Flood the serving plates with the sauce, carefully top with the pork towers, and sprinkle with parsley.

gammon with broad bean and potato pesto salad by james martin

450 g (1 lb) baby new potatoes, halved

225 g (8 oz) frozen broad beans, thawed

1 small red onion, finely chopped

6 tablespoons extra virgin olive oil

2 garlic cloves, crushed

1 teaspoon fresh lemon juice

1 teaspoon balsamic vinegar

1 small French baguette, diagonally sliced

2 x 225 g (8 oz) raw gammon steaks

15 g (½ oz) fresh flatleaf parsley leaves

1 teaspoon fresh oregano leaves

1 canned anchovy fillet, drained and chopped (optional)

40 g (1½ oz) Parmesan wedge

Maldon sea salt and freshly ground black pepper

Fresh basil leaves, to garnish

Ham and peas is a traditional flavour combination which I've brought right up to date with this fantastic spicy dish.

❶ Pre-heat the oven to gas mark 6, 200°C (400°F). Cook the potatoes in boiling salted water for 10–12 minutes until tender, then drain. Blanch the beans in boiling water for 30 seconds, then drain and refresh. Peel away the outer skins and discard them. Place the beans in a bowl and set aside. Add the potatoes when cooked.

❷ Fry the onion in 1 tablespoon of oil for a few minutes until softened. Add 1 garlic clove, the lemon juice, balsamic vinegar and another tablespoon of oil and swirl until combined. Add the bean and potato mixture and stir well. Place over a low heat to keep warm.

❸ Place the bread slices on a baking sheet, drizzle with a little oil and sprinkle with salt. Bake for 5 minutes or until the crostini are crisp but not coloured. Heat a griddle pan. Brush the gammon steaks with a little olive oil and season with pepper. Add to the pan and cook for 2 minutes on each side.

❹ Meanwhile, place the parsley in a food processor with the oregano, anchovy, if using, and remaining garlic, then grate in half of the Parmesan and season to make a pesto. Whizz for about 10 seconds, then pour in the remaining oil and whizz again. Season to taste. Add 2 heaped tablespoons of the parsley pesto to the beans and potatoes and mix well.

❺ Divide the bean and potato mixture between two serving plates. Place the gammon steaks on top and drizzle round the remaining pesto. Scatter over the basil and pare Parmesan shavings on top. Serve with the crostini.

lamb paprika goulash

by brian turner

175 g (6 oz) long-grain rice, well rinsed

2 small lamb neck fillets, trimmed and cut into thin slices

1 dessertspoon paprika

1 tablespoon sunflower oil

50 g (2 oz) unsalted butter

1 onion, finely chopped

50 ml (2 fl oz) dry white wine

1 tablespoon white-wine vinegar

85 ml (3 fl oz) lamb stock

150 ml (5 fl oz) double cream

1 tablespoon chopped fresh flatleaf parsley

4 cocktail gherkins, finely chopped

1 tablespoon chopped fresh mint

Salt and freshly ground black pepper

hot tips

● This dish is almost a stir-fry and the thinner the lamb is cut, the quicker it will cook.

● Traditionally goulash should contain soured cream. This has been specially treated, which makes it thicken slightly and gives it a fresh tang. If you decide to use it instead of double cream, omit the white-wine vinegar from the sauce.

An adaptation of a classic dish, this is great for a special dinner as it can be made in advance and simply reheated gently when needed.

❶ Bring a large pan of salted water to the boil. Add the rice and cook for 10–12 minutes until just tender, then drain well through a sieve.

❷ Toss the lamb in the paprika and season generously. Heat the oil and half the butter in a heavy-based pan and fry the lamb for a couple of minutes until well sealed. Remove from the pan, drain and keep warm.

❸ Add the onion to the lamb pan and cook for 2–3 minutes until softened. Add the wine, wine vinegar, stock and cream. Bring to the boil, then simmer for 3–4 minutes until the liquid is reduced and slightly thickened.

❹ Melt the remaining butter in a frying pan. Add the cooked rice and parsley, season generously and sauté for 1–2 minutes until completely heated through.

❺ Stir the lamb into the cream mixture with the gherkins and mint. Season to taste, stir well to combine and return to a gentle simmer to heat through. Pile the rice on to two serving plates and spoon the lamb over it.

desserts

hot strawberry and raspberry pavlovas   89

plum and almond pizzas   90

banoffee pies   91

apricot tarte tatin with walnut cream   92

coffee and cardamom mushrooms   93

chocolate and pear crème brûlées   94

hot strawberry and raspberry pavlovas by tony tobin

Half a lemon
3 egg whites
1 teaspoon white-wine vinegar
1 teaspoon cornflour
175 g (6 oz) icing sugar, plus 1 tablespoon
1 vanilla pod, seeds only
100 g (4 oz) fresh raspberries
100 g (4 oz) fresh strawberries,
hulled and halved if large
4 tablespoons crème fraîche
Mint sprigs, to decorate

hot tip

● Using icing sugar for meringues produces a smooth, soft, marshmallow texture. If you prefer them with more crunch, use caster sugar. For a crisp outside and soft middle, place the meringues in an oven pre-heated to gas mark 9, 240°C (475°F), then immediately turn it down to gas mark ½, 120°C (250°F) and cook for 1–1½ hours. Leave to go cold and serve with the sauce.

Meringues are really very simple to make and in this recipe they offer a nice change in texture to the strawberry sauce. The extra meringues will keep for two to three weeks in an air-tight container or will freeze for up to six months. Any remaining sauce should be kept covered in the fridge.

❶ Pre-heat the oven to gas mark 7, 220°C (425°F). Grease a baking sheet and line it with parchment paper.

❷ Rub a bowl with the half lemon, add the egg whites and whisk until stiff. Add the vinegar and cornflour, then 175 g (6 oz) of icing sugar, a little at a time, whisking as you go. Then add the vanilla seeds and whisk until very stiff.

❸ Swirl four 15 cm (6 in) shapes on to the lined baking sheet. Cook for 5 minutes on a high shelf, then reduce the oven to gas mark 4, 180°C (350°F). Transfer the meringues to a lower shelf and bake for 6–8 minutes until they are puffed and lightly golden.

❹ Place the raspberries in a liquidizer with the remaining tablespoon of icing sugar and whizz to a purée. Pass through a sieve into a small pan, then add the strawberries to the pan and gently warm through.

❺ Arrange the meringues on serving plates and pour over the raspberry and strawberry sauce. Add a dollop of crème fraîche and decorate with mint sprigs. Serve straight away.

plum and almond pizzas

by tony tobin

50 g (2 oz) unsalted butter
50 g (2 oz) caster sugar
50 g (2 oz) ground almonds
1 egg
½ tablespoon plain flour
1 drop almond essence
2 x 375 g (13 oz) packets ready-rolled puff pastry, thawed if frozen
2 x 400 g (14 oz) can plums in syrup, drained and sliced
4 teaspoons demerara sugar
Vanilla ice-cream, to serve

This is an unusual twist to a very classic combination, although almost any firm fresh or canned fruit would work just as well. Extra pizzas can be frozen for another day. When you're ready to eat them, simply cook as described below, increasing the cooking time by 5–10 minutes.

❶ Pre-heat the oven to gas mark 7, 220°C (425°F). Place the butter and sugar in a food processor and whizz until softened. Add the ground almonds, then the egg and flour. Add the almond essence and whizz again briefly.

❷ Place the pastry sheets on a lightly floured surface and, using a saucer as a template, cut out four 15 cm (6 in) rounds. Place on two baking sheets. Spoon about 2 tablespoons of the almond mixture into the centre of each circle and spread it out, leaving a 1 cm (½ in) space around the edge.

❸ Arrange the plums on top of the almond mixture. Sprinkle 1 teaspoon of demerara sugar over each pizza and bake for 10–12 minutes or until the pizzas are puffed up and golden around the edges. Serve with scoops of vanilla ice-cream.

banoffee pies

by tony tobin

100 g (4 oz) chocolate Hobnobs®
75 g (3 oz) unsalted butter
100 g (4 oz) caster sugar
600 ml (1 pint) double cream
2 large bananas, sliced
100 g (4 oz) bar plain chocolate,
broken into pieces
Sifted cocoa powder and icing sugar,
to decorate

hot tip

● The toffee sauce will keep, covered, in the fridge for a week and is delicious spooned over ice-cream.

This dish is best made 1–2 hours in advance and chilled in the fridge until ready to serve. You can halve the quantities for two people or make four pies and save two for the following night – they are so good, you're bound to want more.

❶ Place the biscuits in a food processor and whizz until they form crumbs. Melt 25 g (1 oz) of butter in a pan. Add the biscuits to the butter and mix until well combined.

❷ Set four, lightly-oiled, 10 cm (4 in) metal cooking rings on plates and divide the biscuit mixture between them, pressing it down firmly to make a base. Push the mixture up around the sides to make a rim to contain the bananas and toffee. Place in the fridge to firm up (or in the freezer if you're short of time).

❸ Heat the sugar gently in a heavy-based pan (not non-stick) until caramelized and toffee-like in colour. Add the remaining butter and half of the cream, and cook over a low heat until the sauce is smooth. Pour into a bowl and place in the fridge to cool. Stir the bananas into half of the sauce. Reserve the remaining sauce for handing round with the pies later.

❹ Melt the chocolate in a heatproof bowl set over a pan of simmering water. Cool slightly. Lightly whip the remaining cream and drizzle in the chocolate. Fold the chocolate through the cream to create a ripple effect.

❺ Carefully remove the rings from around the biscuit bases and put the pies on serving plates. Spoon over the banana and toffee mixture, then top with the rippled cream. Dust around each plate with cocoa powder and icing sugar. Serve with the remaining sauce.

apricot tarte tatin with walnut cream by james martin

2 tablespoons caster sugar
150 ml (5 fl oz) double cream
25 g (1 oz) unsalted butter
375 g (13 oz) packet ready-rolled puff pastry, thawed if frozen
1 small fresh rosemary sprig, leaves removed
400 g (14 oz) can apricot halves in natural juice, drained
1 tablespoon Drambuie liqueur
25 g (1 oz) chopped walnuts
2 tablespoons clear honey
Walnut halves, to decorate

A very stylish-looking dish that's really very easy to make. It provides a spectacular finale to a special dinner. The walnut cream is like an ice-cream and can be made well in advance.

❶ Pre-heat the oven to gas mark 9, 240°C (475°F). Place the caster sugar in a 20 cm (8 in) ovenproof frying pan and heat gently until the sugar dissolves. Stir in 1 tablespoon of cream and the butter and cook for another couple of minutes until the mixture is toffee-like. Remove from the heat.

❷ Place the pastry on a lightly floured work surface and cut out a 23 cm (9 in) circle. Sprinkle the rosemary leaves into the frying pan, then arrange the apricots, cut-side up, on top of them.

❸ Cover the apricots with the pastry, folding the edges down over the sides of the pan for a tight seal. Bake for 10–12 minutes or until the pastry is puffed up and golden.

❹ Meanwhile, place the remaining cream in a bowl and whip until stiff. Fold in the Drambuie, walnuts and honey and chill until ready to use.

❺ Remove the tart from the oven and leave to rest for a minute or so, then invert it on to a serving plate. Just before serving, warm a spoon and scoop some walnut cream into the centre of the tart. Decorate with walnut halves, if liked.

hot tip

● You can ring the changes with this dessert. Try pears, pineapple, bananas or traditional apples. And don't forget fresh herbs, they go surprisingly well with fruit. Rosemary is delicious with pears, and tarragon with apples.

coffee and cardamom mushrooms

by james martin

500 ml (18 fl oz) carton coffee ice-cream
250 ml (9 fl oz) double cream
50 g (2 oz) caster sugar
2 cardamom pods, split
4 egg yolks
2 tablespoons softened unsalted butter
50 g (2 oz) icing sugar, sifted
I egg white
2 tablespoons plain flour
100 g (4 oz) bar milk chocolate, grated
Sifted cocoa powder and
icing sugar, to decorate

This spectacular dessert may seem a little fiddly but in fact it takes minutes to prepare. The tuiles and custard can both be kept until the next day, for a repeat performance!

❶ Pre-heat the oven to gas mark 7, 220°C (425°F). Line a baking sheet with parchment paper then, using a saucer as a template, mark out six 10 cm (4 in) circles. Line six 120 ml (4 fl oz) dariole moulds with plastic film and fill with the ice-cream. Place in the freezer to refreeze.

❷ Bring the cream, caster sugar and cardamom pods to the boil in a small pan. Remove from the heat and slowly add the egg yolks, then return to the heat and cook gently until the mixture coats the back of a spoon. Sieve the custard into a jug and place in the fridge to set.

❸ Make the tuiles: place the butter and icing sugar in a food processor and process until softened, then, with the motor running, slowly add the egg white, followed by the flour. Place a little of the mixture in the centre of each circle on the baking sheet and spread out thinly to cover. Don't worry if the mixture makes more tuiles than you need, they can be kept until the next day and are delicious served with ice-cream or any other creamy dessert. Bake the tuiles for 2–3 minutes or until lightly coloured, then immediately remove from the paper with a spatula and mould them over egg cups. Leave to set.

❹ Sprinkle the grated chocolate around the edges of the serving plates. Turn out an ice-cream into the middle of each plate. Spoon around the cardamom custard and place a shaped tuile upside-down on top of the ice-cream. Dust with cocoa powder and icing sugar.

chocolate and pear crème brûlées

by james martin

200 ml (7 fl oz) milk
300 ml (10 fl oz) double cream
50 g (2 oz) caster sugar
2 tablespoons cocoa powder, sifted
100 g (4 oz) bar plain chocolate,
broken into pieces
7 egg yolks
1 tablespoon dark rum
400 g (14 oz) can pear halves in syrup,
drained and patted dry
2 tablespoons demerara sugar
Fresh mint sprigs, to decorate

hot tips

● Sprinkle with sugar just before grilling and always use demerara sugar which forms a lovely thin crust.
● You could also use fresh pears, when in season, for this recipe.

Pears and chocolate are a classic combination and with a measure of rum you're guaranteed a dessert to die for. Without the brûlée topping, these will keep in the fridge for up to 24 hours, so you can come back again and again.

❶ Place the milk, cream and caster sugar in a small pan and bring to the boil. Remove from the heat, add the cocoa powder and chocolate pieces and whisk until the chocolate has melted.

❷ Pour the chocolate mixture on to the egg yolks and blend together. Return the mixture to the pan, stir in the rum and cook gently until the mixture coats the back of a spoon. Pour the sauce through a sieve into a bowl.

❸ Slice half the pears and arrange them in the bottom of six 120 ml (4 fl oz) ramekins. Fill the ramekins with the chocolate mixture and place in the fridge to set (or in the freezer if you're short of time).

❹ Pre-heat the grill to very hot. Sprinkle the chocolate pots with demerara sugar and flash under the grill to caramelize. (Alternatively, you could use a blow torch, but you must be extremely careful not to burn your hands.) Fan out the remaining pear halves and sprinkle them with demerara sugar. Grill until caramelized and serve with the brûlées. Decorate with mint sprigs.